MAPPING YOUR FINANCIAL FUTURE

Setting Clear Financial Goals

Ann Bost

CONTENTS

FOREWORD

Dear Readers,

I am absolutely thrilled and grateful for the overwhelming response to my first book, "Unleash Your Financial Brilliance." Your support and enthusiasm have inspired me to continue this journey of empowerment and financial growth together.

As I delved into the topics of mindset, self-discovery, and financial transformation in "Unleash Your Financial Brilliance," I realized that there is so much more I want to share with you. The seeds of a new idea were sown, and today, I am thrilled to introduce the "Financial Freedom Series."
This series is dedicated to empowering ambitious business women, just like you, with the knowledge and tools to achieve financial independence and freedom. Through each book in the series, we will explore essential aspects of financial education, motivation, and empowerment, guiding you on your path to financial success.

In the following months, you can look forward to delving into topics such as setting clear financial goals, crafting personalized financial plans, building a supportive network, investing in financial education, and much more. Each book in the series is designed to equip you with practical strategies, actionable steps, and an abundance mindset to create lasting financial prosperity.
I am beyond excited to embark on this journey with you and create a thriving community of empowered women. Stay tuned for the launch of each book, and together, let's unleash our financial brilliance and build a life of abundance and success.

Thank you for being part of this incredible adventure, and remember, the best is yet to come!

With gratitude and excitement,

Ann Bost

P.S : *Don't forget to check out the first book in the series, "Unleash Your Financial Brilliance," available in both paperback and ebook formats. Let's continue to grow, learn, and thrive together*

INTRODUCTION

Welcome to the second book in the "Financial Freedom Series" - "Mapping Your Financial Future: Setting Clear Financial Goals." I am thrilled to continue this transformative journey with you, empowering business ambitious women like yourself to take control of your financial destiny.

In this empowering guide, we will delve into the power of setting clear and achievable financial goals, a crucial step on the path to financial freedom. Building upon the foundation laid in "Unleash Your Financial Brilliance," we will now focus on crafting a concrete financial roadmap that aligns your aspirations with actionable strategies. As an ambitious businesswoman, you know that success requires direction, determination, and a powerful vision.

In this book, we will help you define that vision, connect it to your financial goals, and chart a course towards the life you desire. Setting clear financial goals is not just about numbers; it's about unlocking the potential within yourself and building the life you deserve.

Whether your dreams include starting a thriving business, achieving financial independence, or making a lasting impact in your community, this guide will equip you with the tools to turn those aspirations into reality.

As we navigate through the chapters, we'll explore goal-setting strategies, assess your current financial situation, and create a personalized financial roadmap tailored to your unique aspirations and circumstances.

Remember, financial empowerment is within your grasp. I invite you to embrace this journey wholeheartedly and rewrite your financial story. By setting clear financial goals and taking inspired action, you can build a glass empire that knows no limits.

Let's embark on this empowering adventure together as we map out your financial future and unlock the boundless potential that lies within you.

CHAPTER 1
THE POWER OF VISION

In this transformative chapter, we will delve into the immense power of having a clear vision for your financial future.

Just like a skilled architect creates a blueprint before constructing a magnificent building, envisioning your financial dreams is the first step towards building a life of abundance and success.

Section 1
Envisioning Your Ideal Life

Step 1: Reflect on Your Passions and Values

Welcome to the first step of your transformative financial journey! In this chapter, we will explore the power of aligning your financial goals with your deepest passions and core values. By connecting your aspirations with your authentic self, you will unlock a sense of purpose that will fuel your path towards financial brilliance.

Why Reflect on Your Passions and Values?

Your passions and values are the compass that guides you through life's journey. When it comes to financial success, understanding what truly matters to you is the key to setting meaningful goals. By reflecting on your passions, you gain insight into what brings you joy, fulfillment, and purpose. Your values, on the other hand, define your moral compass and what you stand for. When your financial goals align with your passions and values, every step you take becomes purposeful and fulfilling.

The Journey of Self-Discovery

Take a moment to embark on a journey of self-discovery. Dive deep into your inner self and explore the activities that light up your soul and the causes that ignite your passion.

Ask yourself:

- What activities do I enjoy the most?
- What brings me a sense of purpose and fulfillment?
- What values do I hold dear, and how do they impact my decision-making?

Connecting with your passions and values is not only a powerful exercise for financial growth but also a transformative experience that aligns every aspect of your life with your authentic self.

Creating Your Vision Board

Now that you have a clearer understanding of your passions and values, let's take it a step further. Create a vision board that visually represents your financial dreams and aspirations. Use images, words, and symbols that resonate with your core desires. Your vision board will serve as a constant reminder of your true purpose, keeping you motivated and focused on the path to financial success.

Setting Aligned Financial Goals

As you reflect on your passions and values, you will gain valuable insights into the financial goals that truly matter to you. Set bold, specific, and aligned goals that connect with your vision and purpose. These goals will be the stepping stones that lead you towards financial empowerment and abundance.

Remember, reflecting on your passions and values is not just a one-time exercise. It is a continuous journey of self-awareness and growth. As you progress through this book, keep revisiting your passions and values, ensuring that your financial decisions align with your authentic self.

Unlock the power within you by harnessing the energy of your passions and values. Embrace your true self and create a financial future that reflects your deepest desires and aspirations. Your journey towards financial brilliance starts with this first step, and together, we will pave the way for your extraordinary success.

Step 2 : Visualize Your Ideal Lifestyle

Congratulations on taking the second step towards unlocking your financial brilliance! In this chapter, we will delve into the art of visualization, a powerful tool that will bring your financial dreams to life. As you close your eyes and embrace your ideal lifestyle, you will begin to see the limitless possibilities that await you.

The Power of Visualization

Visualization is the process of using your imagination to create a vivid mental image of your desired reality. It goes beyond wishful thinking; it is a transformative practice that taps into the immense power of your subconscious mind. When you visualize your ideal lifestyle, you activate the Law of Attraction, attracting opportunities and resources that align with your vision.

Creating Your Ideal Lifestyle

Close your eyes and take a deep breath. Transport yourself to a future where your financial dreams have come true. Imagine waking up in the house of your dreams, a space that reflects your personality and brings you a profound sense of comfort. Visualize yourself surrounded by loved ones, cherishing moments of joy and togetherness.

Envision yourself exploring exotic destinations, soaking in the wonders of the world and creating unforgettable memories. Picture the financial security that allows you to pursue your passions, engage in fulfilling activities, and give back to the causes that resonate with your heart.

Embrace the Emotions

As you visualize your ideal lifestyle, embrace the emotions that accompany this vision. Feel the excitement, the sense of achievement, and the freedom that come with financial success. Let these emotions flow through you, igniting your determination to turn this vision into reality.

Aligning with Your Vision

Your visualization is not just a daydream; it is a blueprint for your financial journey. With every mental image you create, you are setting intentions and aligning your actions with your dreams. Use your visualization practice as a source of inspiration, especially during challenging times. When you face obstacles, revisit your ideal lifestyle, and let it remind you of the limitless potential within you.

Turning Dreams into Action

Your visualization practice will be the driving force behind your actions. As you proceed through this book, you will learn practical strategies and tools to transform your vision into actionable steps. Your ideal lifestyle is within reach, and with every chapter, you will come closer to manifesting it.

Take a moment to thank yourself for embarking on this transformative journey. You have the power to design your ideal lifestyle, and it starts with the power of visualization. Embrace this practice, and let it illuminate your path towards financial freedom and extraordinary success.

Remember, you are the architect of your life, and your vision will guide you towards a future filled with abundance and prosperity. Embrace the power of visualization and step confidently towards the life you've always dreamed of.

Step 3: Set Bold and Specific Goals

Are you ready to turn your financial dreams into actionable reality? In Step 3 of "Mapping Your Financial Future: Setting Clear Financial Goals," we dive into the transformative power of setting bold and specific financial goals. Your aspirations are within reach, and I'm here to provide actionable steps and valuable insights to help you achieve them.

- **Plotting Your Financial Coordinates**

Just like a skilled navigator plotting coordinates on a map, setting clear and specific financial goals will guide you towards the life of abundance and success you desire. Without goals, you risk drifting aimlessly, unsure of your progress and lacking the motivation to reach your dreams.

To effectively plot your financial coordinates, follow these steps:

1. Assess Your Current Financial Situation:

Start by taking stock of your current financial situation. Review your income, expenses, assets, and debts. This will give you a clear picture of where you stand financially and serve as a foundation for setting your goals.

2. Define Your Financial Vision:

Envision your ideal financial future and what it looks like to you. What are your long-term dreams and aspirations? Having a clear vision will help you set more meaningful and achievable goals.

3. Set Specific and Measurable Goals:

Break down your financial vision into specific and measurable goals. For example, if you want to save for a down payment on a house, determine how much money you need to save and by what date.

4. Prioritize Your Goals:

Identify which goals are most important to you and prioritize them. This will help you focus your efforts and resources on what matters most.

5. Create a Timeline:

Establish a timeline for each goal. Determine when you want to achieve each goal and set realistic deadlines. This will provide a sense of urgency and keep you on track.

6. Identify Actionable Steps:

Break down each goal into actionable steps. What specific actions do you need to take to reach your goals? Write down the steps and create a plan to follow through.

7. Monitor Your Progress:

Regularly review your progress towards your goals. Track your financial growth and celebrate milestones along the way. Adjust your plan if necessary to stay on course.

8. Stay Accountable:

Share your goals with someone you trust, like a friend or family member, to hold yourself accountable. Having someone to support and encourage you can make a significant difference in staying motivated.

9. Seek Professional Guidance:

If you're unsure about financial planning or investment strategies, consider consulting a financial advisor. A professional can provide personalized advice and help you make informed decisions.

10. Stay Committed:

Achieving financial goals takes time and effort. Stay committed to your vision and remind yourself regularly of why you're working towards these goals. Keep your vision alive and visualize your success regularly.

By following these steps and plotting your financial coordinates, you'll have a clear roadmap to guide you towards financial success and a brighter future. Remember, it's essential to be patient and persistent, as financial planning is a journey that requires dedication and discipline. But with determination and the right strategies, you can achieve your financial dreams and create the life you desire.

- **Defining Your Financial Aspirations**

What does financial freedom mean to you? How much wealth do you want to accumulate? In this step, you'll define your financial aspirations with confidence, embracing the belief that you have the power to achieve them.
To define your financial aspirations and set meaningful goals, consider the following tips and insights:

- Explore Your Deepest Desires:

Take the time to delve into your deepest desires and dreams. What does financial freedom mean to you? Is it about having the flexibility to travel the world, starting your dream business, or securing a comfortable retirement? Knowing what truly matters to you will fuel your motivation and commitment to achieving your goals.

- Be Specific and Realistic:

As you define your financial aspirations, be specific and realistic about what you want to achieve. Setting overly vague or unattainable goals can lead to frustration and disappointment. Instead, break down your aspirations into tangible and achievable targets.

- Quantify Your Goals:

Assigning specific numbers to your goals makes them more concrete. For example, if you aim to build an emergency fund, decide on an exact amount you want to save, like three to six months' worth of living expenses.

- Consider Short-term and Long-term Goals:

While long-term goals are essential for envisioning your financial future, don't neglect short-term objectives. Having smaller milestones along the way will help you maintain focus and celebrate progress more frequently.

- Align Your Goals with Values:

Ensure that your financial aspirations align with your core values and beliefs. When your goals resonate with your values, they become more meaningful and fulfilling.

- Visualize Your Success:

Close your eyes and visualize yourself achieving your financial aspirations. Feel the excitement, joy, and pride that come with accomplishing each goal. Visualization can be a powerful tool in staying motivated and committed to your journey.

- Stay Flexible and Open-Minded:

Life is full of unexpected twists and turns. Stay open to adjusting your goals if circumstances change. Flexibility allows you to adapt and seize new opportunities that align with your aspirations.

- Break Down Large Goals:

If your financial aspirations seem overwhelming, break them down into smaller, manageable steps. Tackling smaller tasks will make your goals feel more attainable and less daunting.

- Celebrate Progress:

Celebrate every milestone you achieve, no matter how big or small. Celebrations serve as positive reinforcement and remind you of the progress you've made.

- Track Your Financial Growth:

Keep a record of your financial growth and monitor your progress regularly. Tracking your success will inspire confidence and encourage you to continue pushing forward.

Defining your financial aspirations is a pivotal step in your journey towards financial empowerment. Remember that your aspirations are unique to you, and there is no one-size-fits-all approach. Embrace your dreams, set your goals with intention, and stay committed to the transformative path ahead. With dedication and the right mindset, you have the power to turn your financial aspirations into reality.

- **Making Goals Specific and Measurable**

Vague goals lack the power to inspire and motivate. Instead, make your goals specific and measurable. Define the exact amount you want to save, invest, or earn, and set a timeline for each milestone.

Setting clear and specific financial goals is the key to turning your dreams into actionable reality. As you embark on your journey towards financial freedom, let's explore how to make your goals specific and measurable, empowering you to track your progress and stay motivated.

1. Define the Exact Amount:

Instead of saying, "I want to save more money," be precise about the amount you want to save. For example, "I aim to save $10,000 in the next six months." This clarity will give you a clear target to work towards.

2. Set a Timeline:

Assign a specific timeframe to each goal. Determine when you want to achieve your financial milestones. Having a deadline creates a sense of urgency and helps you stay focused.

3. Break It Down:

Divide big goals into smaller, manageable steps. If your ultimate goal is to buy a house, outline the steps needed, such as saving for a down payment, researching mortgage options, and setting a timeline for the purchase.

4. Use Numbers and Metrics:

Incorporate numbers and metrics to measure your progress. Track your savings, investments, or debt reduction in real numbers to see the impact of your efforts.

5. Assess Your Progress:

Regularly review your goals and assess your progress. Celebrate the milestones you achieve, and if necessary, make adjustments to stay on track.

6. Stay Accountable:

Share your goals with someone you trust, like a friend or mentor, who can help keep you accountable and provide support on your journey.

By making your financial goals specific and measurable, you'll gain a clear roadmap to navigate your financial future. This approach empowers you to take actionable steps towards achieving your dreams, making financial success within your reach.

Remember, each small step you take brings you closer to your vision of financial abundance and creates a lasting impact on your life. Stay committed, stay focused, and you'll unlock your true financial brilliance. Let's make your financial goals a reality together!

- **Creating a Roadmap**

Your goals will become the roadmap that leads you to your desired destination. Each milestone is a stepping stone towards your dreams, and we'll break down large goals into smaller, manageable steps.

- **Visualizing Success**

Embrace the emotions of success, and visualize yourself achieving your financial goals. Picture the joy, pride, and sense of accomplishment that come with each milestone. Let these emotions fuel your determination to persevere.

- **Staying Adaptable**

While setting clear goals is essential, staying adaptable is equally crucial. Life is full of surprises, and your goals may need adjustments along the way. Embrace change as an opportunity for growth and keep your eyes on the prize.

Conclusion

As we move forward in this book, I'll equip you with the tools, insights, and guidance to turn your financial goals into reality. Your journey towards financial freedom is not just about reaching the destination; it's about the transformation and growth you experience along the way. Together, let's set sail towards your dreams, one goal at a time. The path to financial success is within your reach, and with each step, you'll move closer to unlocking your full potential and creating a life of abundance and success. Let's embark on this transformative journey together!

Step 4: Align Your Vision with Your Purpose

Congratulations on setting clear and specific financial goals! As we continue our journey in "Mapping Your Financial Future," we now dive into the transformative power of aligning your financial vision with your purpose. When your goals are driven by a higher sense of purpose and passion, you unleash the true potential of your financial journey.

Your vision should align with your purpose and sense of mission. Ask yourself how your financial success can positively impact others and contribute to the greater good. When your vision is driven by purpose, you will find unwavering determination to pursue your goals.

- **Discovering Your Why:**

Take a moment to reflect on your life's purpose and the impact you want to create.

Ask yourself why achieving financial success is essential to you.

How will it contribute to your sense of purpose and the greater good?

When it comes to aligning your financial vision with your purpose, understanding your "why" is the foundation of your journey. Your "why" represents the deeper reason behind your financial goals – the driving force that fuels your passion, determination, and commitment to achieving them. Here are some detailed examples to help you discover your "why":

Example 1: Building a Secure Future for Your Family

Your "why" might be rooted in creating a secure and abundant future for your family. Perhaps you envision providing your children with the best education, offering them opportunities you didn't have, and ensuring they have a solid foundation to pursue their dreams. Your financial success becomes a means to secure your family's well-being and happiness.

Example 2: Fulfilling Your Life's Purpose

Your "why" could be driven by a deep sense of purpose and the desire to make a difference in the world. You may have a passion for a specific cause, such as environmental conservation or social justice, and see your financial success as a tool to support and drive positive change in those areas.

Example 3: Achieving Personal Freedom and Independence

Your "why" might be centered around achieving personal freedom and independence. Perhaps you dream of breaking free from financial constraints, escaping the 9-to-5 grind, and having the flexibility to pursue your passions and interests on your terms.

Example 4: Leaving a Lasting Legacy

Your "why" could be about leaving a lasting legacy. You may envision building a successful business, creating a charitable foundation, or leaving behind a body of work that positively impacts future generations.

Example 5: Overcoming Past Financial Struggles

Your "why" might be born out of past financial struggles or setbacks.
You may be determined to break free from limiting beliefs and create a new financial narrative for yourself and your family.

Example 6: Empowering Others through Financial Education

Your "why" could be focused on empowering others through financial education and mentorship. You may have a passion for helping others achieve financial literacy and success, and your own financial journey becomes a source of inspiration for others.

Take the time to reflect on these examples and identify the one that resonates most with you. Your "why" will be unique to your life experiences, values, and aspirations. Embrace your "why" as a powerful motivator on your financial journey, and let it guide you towards achieving your goals with purpose and passion. Remember, understanding your "why" is a transformative step towards aligning your financial vision with your true purpose in life.

- **Connecting Your Goals to Your Values:**

Ensure that your financial goals align with your core values. For example, if you value giving back to the community, consider incorporating charitable donations or social impact investing into your financial plan.

- **Finding Meaning in Your Financial Journey:**

Shift your focus from merely accumulating wealth to finding meaning in your financial journey. Embrace the sense of fulfillment that comes from knowing your financial success is contributing to your purpose and leaving a positive legacy.

- **Overcoming Challenges with Purpose:**

When you encounter challenges on your path to financial success, your sense of purpose will fuel your determination to overcome them. Embrace setbacks as opportunities for growth and use your purpose as a guiding light.

- **Balancing Ambition and Meaning:**

Strive to strike a balance between ambition and meaning. While it's essential to have ambitious financial goals, ensure they are in harmony with your purpose, values, and overall well-being.

- **Creating Lasting Impact:**

Remember that your financial journey is not just about accumulating wealth for yourself but also about creating a lasting impact on the world. Embrace the opportunity to make a difference through your financial choices.

Conclusion

As you align your financial vision with your purpose, you'll discover a newfound sense of fulfillment and motivation on your journey. Your financial success will transcend beyond the numbers, becoming a powerful tool to make a positive impact on your life and the lives of others.

Together, let's continue mapping your financial future with purpose, passion, and a clear vision. By aligning your goals with your purpose, you'll unleash the true potential of your financial brilliance and create a life of abundance and significance.

Let's move forward with purpose, as we embark on this transformative journey together!

Section 2

Defining Your Dreams

Step 1: Prioritize Your Financial Aspirations

Identify the most important financial aspirations from your vision.
What are the key goals that will have the most significant impact on your life?

Prioritize these goals, focusing on the ones that resonate deeply with your desires.

I met a woman named Sarah who embodied the essence of prioritizing her financial aspirations. As a driven and ambitious entrepreneur, Sarah had always dreamed of starting her own eco-friendly fashion brand. However, she faced challenges in finding the resources to turn her dream into a reality.

Sarah began by identifying her core values, which included sustainability, creativity, and empowering others. With these values in mind, she knew that her fashion brand would not only reflect her passion for design but also contribute to a more environmentally conscious world.
She set realistic goals by breaking down her long-term dream into smaller milestones. Initially, Sarah focused on developing a line of sustainable accessories, such as handbags and jewelry, as a stepping stone to her larger vision. This approach allowed her to test the market, build her brand's reputation, and secure funding for future expansion.

Sarah's prioritization process was guided by the impact she wanted to make. She envisioned her fashion brand not just as a business venture but also as a platform to support local artisans and raise awareness about eco-friendly practices in the fashion industry.

As she reviewed and revised her priorities, Sarah sought support and guidance from industry experts and mentors. Their insights and encouragement reaffirmed her commitment to her financial aspirations and gave her the confidence to navigate through challenges.
Throughout her journey, Sarah celebrated every milestone achieved, no matter how small. Each new design launch, positive customer feedback, and media recognition became reasons to rejoice and rekindle her motivation.
Though Sarah's path was not always straightforward, she embraced flexibility and stayed open to seizing opportunities. As her business grew, she explored collaborations with sustainable material suppliers, expanding her impact beyond her brand.

Today, Sarah's eco-friendly fashion brand has become a thriving success. Her story is not just one of financial triumph but also of creating positive change in the world. By prioritizing her financial aspirations aligned with her core values, Sarah turned her dream into a reality, leaving a lasting mark on the fashion industry and inspiring others to do the same.

Sarah's journey illustrates the power of prioritizing financial aspirations and using them as a guiding compass in the pursuit of our dreams. Just like her, you too can shape your financial future by placing your dreams at the forefront and taking intentional steps towards achieving them.
The path to financial brilliance begins with prioritization, and as you set your goals, you'll chart a course that leads to abundance and success.

Step 2: Break Down Long-Term Goals into Short-Term Milestones

While your long-term financial goals are essential, it's equally crucial to break them down into manageable short-term milestones. These milestones will provide a roadmap for your journey and help you stay on track towards your larger aspirations.

In this step, we delve into the art of breaking down your long-term financial goals into manageable short-term milestones. Just like a skilled navigator plots coordinates on a map to reach their destination, breaking down your goals into smaller, achievable steps will pave the way to your financial success.

- The Power of Incremental Progress

Imagine climbing a mountain – it may seem daunting when viewed from the base, but with each step, you make progress towards the summit. Similarly, when you break down your long-term financial goals into smaller milestones, you create a roadmap that allows you to celebrate incremental progress and stay motivated along the way.

- Identifying Milestone Markers

Start by identifying the key milestones that will lead you towards your long-term financial goals. These markers represent significant achievements that, when accomplished, bring you closer to realizing your dreams. Whether it's reaching a certain level of savings, securing a specific investment opportunity, or achieving a targeted revenue milestone, each marker signals progress towards your financial aspirations.

- Setting Realistic Timeframes

Assign realistic timeframes to each milestone to create a sense of urgency and accountability. Be mindful not to overwhelm yourself with unrealistic deadlines. Instead, consider factors such as your current financial situation, resources, and external circumstances when determining the timeline for each step. A well-paced journey ensures that you stay on course and avoid burnout.

- Tracking Your Progress

Maintain a record of your progress towards each milestone. Tracking your achievements not only serves as a motivation booster but also allows you to make informed decisions and adjustments along the way.

Celebrate each milestone you accomplish, acknowledging the effort and dedication that went into achieving it.

- Adapting to the Journey

The journey to financial success is dynamic, and you may encounter unexpected challenges or opportunities. Embrace adaptability as a virtue and remain open to adjusting your course as needed. Sometimes, detours lead to exciting new possibilities and unforeseen growth.

Conclusion

Breaking down your long-term financial goals into short-term milestones is the secret to making progress and staying focused on your journey. By navigating through achievable steps, you'll build momentum and witness your vision becoming a reality one milestone at a time. As we proceed through this ebook, remember that every milestone accomplished brings you closer to the life of abundance and success you desire.

Embrace the power of incremental progress, and together, we'll chart a course that leads to financial brilliance.

Step 3: Quantify Your Financial Goals

Quantify your financial goals with specific numbers and timelines. For example, if your dream is to start your own business, specify the initial investment required, the revenue targets you aim to achieve in the first year, and the timeline for expansion.

In this crucial step, we dive into the art of quantifying your financial goals with specific numbers and timelines. Just like a skilled architect meticulously plans every detail of a building, quantifying your goals provides clarity and direction, setting you on the path to achieving financial success.

- Setting Clear Targets

Quantifying your financial goals involves setting clear and precise targets for your desired outcomes. Whether it's saving for a down payment on your dream home, investing in your business expansion, or building a retirement fund, defining specific numbers and timelines gives your goals substance and purpose.

- Measuring Progress and Success

Having quantifiable goals allows you to track your progress and measure success. Regularly monitor your financial journey, celebrate the milestones achieved, and adjust your strategies when necessary. The ability to measure your advancements fuels motivation and provides valuable insights into your financial decisions.

- Creating a Realistic Plan

Quantifying your financial goals also involves creating a realistic plan that outlines the necessary steps to achieve each target. Break down your goals into smaller, actionable tasks, and prioritize them based on their impact and feasibility. A well-structured plan keeps you organized and focused, ensuring that you stay on course to achieve your financial aspirations.

- Overcoming Challenges

While setting clear targets is essential, it's essential to acknowledge that challenges may arise along the way. Be prepared to face obstacles and embrace them as opportunities for growth. By quantifying your goals and having a well-defined plan, you'll be better equipped to navigate through challenges and find creative solutions.

- Empowering Your Financial Journey

Quantifying your financial goals empowers you to take control of your financial destiny. As you gain a deeper understanding of your objectives, you'll make informed decisions that align with your vision. With each financial goal measured and tracked, you gain confidence in your ability to make meaningful progress.

Conclusion

Quantifying your financial goals breathes life into your aspirations, transforming them from abstract dreams into tangible realities. By setting clear targets, measuring progress, creating a realistic plan, and empowering your journey, you embark on a transformative path towards financial brilliance.

In the following chapters, we'll delve even deeper into the actionable steps and invaluable insights that will guide you to financial freedom and a life of abundance and success. Let's harness the power of quantification, and together, we'll unlock the full potential of your financial future.

Worksheet :

Financial Goals Quantification

Congratulations on taking the first steps towards achieving your financial aspirations! To help you turn your dreams into reality, I've created a powerful exercice to guide you through Step 3: "Quantify Your Financial Goals."

This exercise, we'll dive deeper into quantifying your financial goals to make them more specific and measurable.

Instructions:

1. Review Your Priorities: Take a moment to reflect on the financial aspirations you've identified in Step 1. Which goals are most important to you right now? Consider their impact on your life and rank them in order of priority.

2. Make Your Goals Specific: Refine your financial goals to make them more precise and specific. For example, if one of your aspirations is to save for a down payment on a house, specify the exact amount you need to save and the timeframe to achieve it.

3. Set Measurable Milestones: Break down your long-term goals into smaller, measurable milestones. Define checkpoints along the way to track your progress. This will help you stay motivated and focused as you move towards your larger aspirations.

4. Assign a Timeline: Assign realistic timelines to each of your financial goals and milestones. Setting deadlines will create a sense of urgency and provide a clear timeframe for achieving your dreams.

5. Align Goals with Your Vision: Ensure that your financial goals align with your vision for your ideal life. Your aspirations should be in harmony with your passions, values, and long-term vision of financial freedom.

6. Assess and Adjust: Regularly assess your progress towards your financial goals. If necessary, be open to making adjustments along the way. Life is dynamic, and flexibility is key to staying on course.

7. Celebrate Your Achievements: Celebrate every milestone you achieve, no matter how small. Each step forward is a testament to your determination and progress towards financial brilliance.

Worksheet: Quantify Your Financial Goals

Prioritize Your Financial Aspirations:
Rank your financial goals in order of importance. Consider their impact on your life and determine which ones you'd like to focus on first.

Make Your Goals Specific:
Refine your financial goals to make them more specific and precise. Add details such as exact amounts, percentages, or numbers to quantify your aspirations.

Set Measurable Milestones:
Break down each long-term goal into smaller, measurable milestones. Define checkpoints to track your progress along the way.

Assign a Timeline
Assign realistic timelines to each of your financial goals and milestones. Create a sense of urgency and purpose by setting deadlines for your achievements

Align Goals with Your Vision:
Ensure that your financial goals align with your overall vision for your life. Your aspirations should resonate with your passions, values, and sense of purpose.
Assess and Adjust:
Regularly assess your progress towards your

financial goals. Be open to making adjustments if necessary to stay on track.
Celebrate Your Achievements:
Celebrate every milestone you reach, no matter how small. Acknowledge your growth and progress on your journey towards financial brilliance.

By the end of this exercise, you'll have quantified your financial goals, giving them clarity and direction. Remember that this process is a crucial step towards unlocking your financial potential and creating the life of abundance and success you desire.

Wishing you financial empowerment and fulfillment,

Step 4 : Master the Art of SMART Financial Goals

Welcome to Step 4 of "Mapping Your Financial Future: Setting Clear Financial Goals." In this chapter, we will delve even deeper into the art of SMART financial goals. Building on the valuable insights you gained in "Unleash Your Financial Brilliance," we will equip you with the tools to master the precision, measurability, achievability, relevance, and time-bound nature of SMART goals.

Understanding SMART Goals

The Art of Precision

In this step, we move beyond vague dreams and embrace the power of specificity. Picture yourself standing at the pinnacle of your financial success – what do you see? Whether it's owning a luxurious beachfront property, launching your own thriving business, or achieving a specific level of financial independence, let every aspiration be defined with crystal-clear clarity. Specificity fuels your motivation, keeps you focused, and paves the way for remarkable achievements.

Insight: As you define your financial goals with precision, visualize the life you desire down to the finest details. Imagine how it feels to live your dreams – the sights, sounds, and emotions that come with financial success. The more vividly you picture your future, the more real and achievable it becomes.

Measurability: Numbers That Tell a Story

Transform your dreams into quantifiable targets that resonate with your inner financial architect. Every financial goal should speakthe language of numbers.

How much do you want to save, invest, or earn?
What is the precise timeline you've set for achieving each milestone?

As you quantify your goals, they become tangible and actionable. Witness the power of measurable objectives as they breathe life into your financial journey, allowing you to track progress, celebrate victories, and adjust your course with precision.

Insight: Turn your financial goals into specific numerical values that you can track and evaluate regularly. Create a financial dashboard or spreadsheet to monitor your progress, showcasing the steady advancement towards your objectives. Celebrate each financial milestone reached, as each step brings you closer to the life you envision.

Achievability: Striving for Brilliance, One Step at a Time

In this section, we strike the perfect balance between ambition and reality. While reaching for the stars, it's crucial to remain grounded in your present capabilities and resources. Together, we'll explore the delicate art of setting achievable goals that stretch your limits without overwhelming you. This chapter will equip you with the tools to assess your strengths, navigate challenges, and turn audacious dreams into attainable triumphs.

Insight: Break down your long-term financial goals into smaller, achievable steps. Each step becomes a building block for your financial success, and as you conquer one milestone, the next becomes more accessible. Celebrate your progress along the way, acknowledging the effort and dedication you invest in your financial journey.

Relevance: Where Purpose Meets Prosperity.

Discover the extraordinary synergy between your life's purpose and your financial ambitions. Unleash the immense potential of aligning your goals with your deepest values and aspirations. Your financial journey becomes a powerful expression of your life's purpose, infused with a profound sense of meaning and fulfillment. Let your financial pursuits be driven by relevance, and witness how purpose and prosperity intertwine to create a life of harmony and impact.

Insight: Reflect on how your financial goals align with your values and sense of purpose. Consider how achieving these goals will positively impact your life and the lives of others. As you infuse your financial journey with purpose, your passion and commitment will propel you forward, even in challenging times.

Time-bound: The Rhythm of Progress

In this section, we embrace the essence of time-bound goals, assigning deadlines that ignite a sense of urgency and determination. Your dreams come alive as you set specific timeframes for each milestone, ensuring that your financial journey remains on track. With the passage of time, witness your aspirations transform into reality, driven by your unwavering commitment and passion.

Insight: Create a financial timeline that outlines when you aim to achieve each specific goal. Set both short-term and long-term deadlines to keep your financial roadmap on track. Remember that time is a valuable resource, and setting time-bound goals empowers you to make the most of it on your journey towards financial success.

As we conclude this chapter, you have mastered the art of SMART financial goals. By embracing specificity, measurability, achievability, relevance, and time-bound nature, you've equipped yourself with a powerful toolset to turn your financial dreams into actionable reality. With each step, you move closer to unlocking your full financial potential and creating a life of abundance and success. Let the rhythm of progress guide you, and together, we'll continue mapping your financial future with brilliance and purpose.

CHAPTER 2
BUILDING A SOLID FOUNDATION

Welcome to Chapter 2 of "Mapping Your Financial Future: Setting Clear Financial Goals." In this chapter, we'll focus on building a solid financial foundation to support your journey towards financial freedom. By assessing your current financial situation and identifying potential obstacles, you'll be better prepared to navigate the path ahead.

Section 1

Assessing Your Financial Situation

In this section,we'll dive into a comprehensive assessment of your current financial situation. By understanding where you stand financially, you'll gain valuable insights into your strengths and areas that need improvement. This assessment will serve as the groundwork for setting realistic and achievable financial goals.

- Evaluating Your Assets and Liabilities

Take an inventory of your assets and liabilities, including savings, investments, debts, and other financial commitments. Understanding your financial standing will provide clarity on the steps needed to secure your financial future.

- Analyzing Income and Expenses

Track your income and expenses to identify patterns and areas where you can make adjustments. Effective budgeting and expense management are key to optimizing your financial resources.

- Assessing Risk Tolerance

Understand your risk tolerance and attitude towards investment opportunities. This knowledge will guide you in making informed decisions that align with your financial objectives.

- Analyzing Income and Expenses

Track your income and expenses to identify patterns and areas where you can make adjustments. Effective budgeting and expense management are key to optimizing your financial resources.

In today's fast-paced world, managing your finances with clarity and purpose is essential to achieving your financial goals. In this section, we'll delve deeper into the crucial task of "Analyzing Income and Expenses" – a foundational step in understanding your financial landscape and making informed decisions for a prosperous future.

Step 1: Organize Your Financial Records

Gather all your financial records, including pay stubs, bank statements, credit card bills, and receipts. Create a comprehensive snapshot of your financial transactions over the past few months. This organized view will give you valuable insights into your spending habits and income streams.

Step 2: Categorize Your Expenses

Break down your expenses into categories such as housing, utilities, transportation, groceries, entertainment, and savings. Categorizing your expenses will help you identify which areas consume most of your income and where there is room for optimization.

Step 3: Calculate Your Total Income

Sum up all your sources of income, including salary, bonuses, freelance work, or any other monetary inflows. Understanding your total income is vital for effective budgeting and financial planning.

Step 4: Assess Your Spending Habits

Analyze your spending patterns to identify areas of discretionary spending and non-essential expenses. Pinpoint areas where you can cut back or find more cost-effective alternatives without compromising on your quality of life.

Step 5: Create a Budget

Develop a realistic and achievable budget that aligns with your financial goals. Allocate a portion of your income to essential expenses, savings, investments, and debt repayment. A well-crafted budget serves as a powerful tool for financial discipline and enables you to direct your money towards what truly matters.

Step 6: Identify Opportunities for Savings

Through careful analysis, you'll uncover opportunities for savings. Consider negotiating bills, cutting subscription costs, or refinancing loans to lower interest rates. Small changes in your spending habits can add up to significant savings over time.

Step 7: Evaluate Your Debt Situation

Assess your outstanding debts, including credit card balances, loans, and mortgages. Prioritize repayment strategies to reduce high-interest debts and avoid accumulating unnecessary interest expenses.

Step 8: Set Financial Goals

Now that you have a clear understanding of your financial situation, set specific financial goals based on your aspirations and values. Whether it's building an emergency fund, saving for a dream vacation, or paying off student loans, having well-defined goals will keep you motivated and on track.

Step 9: Regularly Review and Adjust

Financial situations evolve over time, so it's essential to regularly review and adjust your budget and financial goals. Set aside time each month to assess your progress, celebrate achievements, and make necessary changes to your financial plan.

Analyzing your income and expenses is the cornerstone of financial empowerment. Armed with a comprehensive understanding of your financial landscape, you have the power to optimize your resources, make informed decisions, and work towards a more prosperous future. Remember, taking control of your finances is an ongoing journey, and with determination and dedication, you can create a life of financial freedom and abundance.

- Assessing Risk Tolerance

Understand your risk tolerance and attitude towards investment opportunities. This knowledge will guide you in making informed decisions that align with your financial objectives.

Assessing Risk Tolerance:

Your Path to Informed Financial Decisions

In the pursuit of financial success, understanding your risk tolerance is a pivotal aspect of your journey. In this chapter, we explore the crucial concept of "Assessing Risk Tolerance" and how it influences your investment decisions and financial objectives. By gaining clarity on your risk appetite and attitude towards investment opportunities, you will be better equipped to navigate the complex world of finance with confidence and purpose.

Step 1: Define Your Risk Tolerance

Reflect on your comfort level when faced with financial risks. Are you more inclined towards conservative and low-risk investments, or do you embrace a more adventurous approach seeking higher returns? Understanding your risk tolerance is a key factor in developing a personalized investment strategy that aligns with your unique financial goals and circumstances.

Step 2: Assess Your Financial Goals

Consider your short-term and long-term financial goals. Are you aiming for steady growth and preservation of capital, or are you open to higher volatility in pursuit of substantial gains? By aligning your risk tolerance with your specific financial objectives, you can strike a balance between prudence and ambition.

Step 3: Evaluate Your Time Horizon

Take into account your investment time horizon, which refers to the duration you plan to hold your investments. A longer time horizon often allows for a more diversified portfolio and may afford you the opportunity to ride out market fluctuations. On the other hand, a shorter time horizon may require a more conservative investment approach to protect capital.

Step 4: Consider Your Financial Situation

Assess your current financial situation, including your income, expenses, and existing investments. Understanding your overall financial health will help you make well-informed decisions regarding the level of risk you are comfortable assuming in your investment portfolio.

Step 5: Conduct a Risk Tolerance

Questionnaire Consider using a risk tolerance questionnaire to gain deeper insights into your attitude towards risk. These questionnaires are designed to evaluate your emotional response to market fluctuations and assess your willingness to tolerate potential losses. The results will provide valuable guidance for your investment decisions.

Step 6: Seek Professional Guidance

If you find assessing your risk tolerance challenging or feel overwhelmed by the intricacies of investments, consider consulting a financial advisor. An experienced advisor can provide expert insights, help you define your risk profile, and tailor a suitable investment strategy that aligns with your goals.

Step 7: Diversify Your Portfolio

Diversification is a fundamental risk management strategy that involves spreading your investments across various asset classes and industries. This approach can help reduce the impact of market volatility and protect your portfolio against significant losses.

Assessing your risk tolerance is an essential step in your financial journey. By understanding your comfort level with risk and aligning it with your financial goals, you can build a resilient and purposeful investment portfolio. Remember, there is no one-size-fits-all approach to risk tolerance, and your investment strategy should be as unique as you are. Armed with this knowledge, you are now equipped to make informed decisions that pave the way towards achieving your financial objectives and creating lasting wealth.

Worksheet

Assessing Your Financial Situation

This worksheet will guide you through a comprehensive assessment of your current financial situation. Take your time and be honest with your answers. Understanding where you stand financially will provide valuable insights for setting realistic and achievable financial goals.

Part 1: Evaluating Your Assets and Liabilities

1. List Your Assets:

2. Cash and Savings:

    ____

3. Investments (stocks, bonds, mutual funds, etc.):

    ____

4. Retirement Accounts (401(k), IRA, etc.):

    ____

5. Real Estate Properties:

    ____

6. Other Assets (vehicles, valuable possessions, etc.):

7. Calculate Your Total Assets:

____

8. List Your Liabilities (Debts):

- Credit Card Debt:

____

- Student Loans:

____

- Mortgage:

____

- Personal Loans:

____

- Other Debts:

____

9. Calculate Your Total Liabilities:

____

10. Calculate Your Net Worth (Total Assets - Total Liabilities):

____

Part 2: Analyzing Income and Expenses

1. List Your Total Monthly Income (after taxes):

____

2. List Your Total Monthly Expenses:

- Housing (rent/mortgage, utilities, property taxes):

  ____

- Transportation (car payments, insurance, gas, public transport):

  ____

- Food (groceries, dining out):

  ____

- Health and Insurance (healthcare, insurance premiums):

  ____

- Entertainment and Recreation:

  ____

- Debt Payments:

  ____

- Savings and Investments:

  ____

- Other Expenses:

  ____

3. Calculate Your Total Monthly Expenses:

  ____

4. Calculate Your Monthly Disposable Income (Total Income - Total Expenses):

  ____

Part 3: Assessing Risk Tolerance

1. How would you describe your risk
    tolerance when it comes to investments?

    *   Low (Prefer safe and stable
        investments)

    *   Moderate (Comfortable with a mix of
        risk and reward)

    *   High (Willing to take on higher risk for
        potentially higher returns)

2. Are you currently investing in any stocks,
    mutual funds, or other investment
    vehicles? If yes, please list them and
    their approximate value:

    ____

Part 4: Summary and Reflection

What insights have you gained from
completing this assessment?

____

____

____

Based on your current financial situation, what are the key areas you'd like to improve or focus

____

____

____

Remember, this assessment is a starting point for your financial journey.

By understanding your current financial standing, you can make informed decisions and set meaningful goals for your future. Use this worksheet as a reference as you move forward with creating your personalized financial plan.

"Discover the power of knowing where you stand to pave the way for where you want to go."

Section 2

Creating a Solid Financial Plan

In this pivotal section, we'll guide you through the process of creating a personalized financial plan. A well-structured plan will serve as your roadmap, outlining the actions and milestones needed to achieve your financial goals.

Let's dive in!

Step 1 Defining Short, Medium, and Long-Term Goals

One of the first steps in creating your financial plan is categorizing your goals into short, medium, and long-term objectives. Take some time to identify what matters most to you and your future. Short-term goals may include building an emergency fund, paying off high-interest debts, or saving for a much-deserved vacation. Medium-term goals could involve saving for a down payment on a house, funding higher education, or launching a new business venture. Long-term goals might revolve around retirement planning, achieving financial independence, or leaving a legacy for your loved ones.

By defining each goal and setting specific timelines for their achievement, you'll gain clarity and direction in your financial journey. Prioritizing these goals will help you allocate resources effectively and maintain focus as you work towards your aspirations. Remember, the key is to make these goals both ambitious and realistic, inspiring you to take action while acknowledging the necessary steps to reach them.

At the end of this chapter 2, I invite you to take action and define your short, medium, and long-term financial goals. To help you through this process, I've prepared the 'Defining Short, Medium, and Long-Term Goals' worksheet. This valuable resource will guide you step-by-step in setting clear and specific financial objectives. By completing this worksheet, you'll create a personalized roadmap to financial success. I encourage you to take the time to reflect on your aspirations and prioritize your goals based on your vision for the future. Remember, each goal you set brings you one step closer to achieving your financial dreams. Let's begin this empowering exercise together!

Step 2: Establishing an Emergency Fund

An emergency fund is a crucial component of any solid financial plan. Life is unpredictable, and unexpected financial challenges can arise at any time. An emergency fund acts as a safety net, providing peace of mind and financial security during difficult times. It is essential to determine the ideal amount for your emergency fund based on your living expenses, financial obligations, and personal circumstances.

In this step, we'll guide you on how to build and maintain your emergency fund. We'll explore strategies to set aside a portion of your income regularly and resist the temptation to dip into it for non-emergencies. By having a robust emergency fund, you'll be prepared for any unforeseen circumstances that may come your way, allowing you to weather financial storms with confidence.

Emergency Fund Building and Maintenance

1. Set Clear Savings Goals:

Determine the target amount you want to have in your emergency fund. Aim for at least three to six months' worth of living expenses. This fund will act as your financial safety net during unforeseen circumstances.

2. Automate Your Savings:

Treat your emergency fund as a non-negotiable expense. Set up automatic transfers from your checking account to a dedicated savings account every time you receive your paycheck. This ensures consistency and discipline in building your fund.

3. Create a Separate Account:

Open a separate savings account specifically for your emergency fund. Keeping it separate from your regular savings prevents you from accidentally using it for non-emergencies.

4. Prioritize Emergency Fund Contributions:

Make contributions to your emergency fund a priority. Even if you start with small amounts, consistent contributions will gradually build up your fund over time.

5. Resist Temptations:

Avoid using your emergency fund for non-emergencies. While it may be tempting to dip into it for unexpected expenses or indulgences, remember that the fund is reserved for genuine emergencies only.

6. Adjust as Needed:

Reevaluate your emergency fund goal periodically, especially when your financial situation changes. If your living expenses increase or decrease, adjust your savings target accordingly.

7. Celebrate Milestones:

Celebrate your progress as you reach milestones in building your emergency fund. Each milestone achieved brings you closer to greater financial security.

Remember, having a well-funded emergency fund provides peace of mind and financial stability, allowing you to navigate unexpected challenges with confidence. Stay committed to building and maintaining your fund, and you'll be better prepared to face whatever life throws your way.

Step 3: Building a Debt Repayment Strategy

Managing and reducing debt is a fundamental aspect of your financial plan. High-interest debts can be a significant financial burden, hindering your progress towards your goals. In this step, we'll show you how to create a strategic debt repayment plan to tackle outstanding debts efficiently.

Start by listing all your debts, including credit cards, loans, and any other outstanding balances. Organize them by interest rates and minimum payments, and identify which debts you should prioritize. In some cases, it may be beneficial to pay off higher-interest debts first to minimize the overall interest paid. Adopting a systematic approach to debt repayment will not only improve your financial health but also free up resources that can be redirected towards achieving your future goals.
Step into the empowering exercise of building a debt repayment strategy.

This transformational process is designed to equip you with the tools and insights needed to take charge of your financial well-being and conquer your outstanding debts with confidence.

In this exercise, we'll embark on a journey of self-discovery and financial empowerment. Together, we'll assess your debts, prioritize repayment, and craft a personalized plan that aligns with your unique financial circumstances. As you progress through this roadmap, you'll not only reduce your debts but also gain valuable knowledge and skills in managing your finances more effectively.

Remember, this journey towards financial freedom requires dedication and determination, but the rewards are immense. By embracing this exercise, you are taking a powerful step towards a debt-free future, one that brings you greater financial flexibility and peace of mind.

Let's embrace the potential of becoming debt-free together, as we unlock the path to a brighter and more prosperous financial future. You've got what it takes, and we're here to guide and support you every step of the way!

Building a Debt Repayment Strategy

1. Take Stock of Your Debts:

Begin by listing all your outstanding debts, including credit card balances, student loans, car loans, and any other loans you may have. Note down the total amount owed, the interest rates, and the minimum monthly payments for each debt.

2. Prioritize High-Interest Debts:

Identify the debts with the highest interest rates. These are the ones that cost you the most in interest over time. Prioritize paying off these high-interest debts first, as doing so will save you money in the long run.

3. Snowball vs. Avalanche Method:

Choose a debt repayment method that suits your financial situation. The snowball method involves paying off the smallest debt first, gaining momentum as you move on to larger debts. The avalanche method focuses on paying off the debt with the highest interest rate first, saving you more money on interest payments.

4. Create a Budget:

Design a budget that allows you to allocate extra funds towards debt repayment. Look for areas where you can cut back on discretionary spending and redirect those funds towards paying off debts.

5. Increase Your Income:

Consider ways to boost your income, such as taking on a part-time job, freelancing, or selling items you no longer need. The additional income can accelerate your debt repayment progress.

6. Negotiate Lower Interest Rates:

Contact your creditors to inquire about the possibility of reducing interest rates. Some credit card companies and lenders may be willing to negotiate lower rates, which can help you pay off your debts faster.

7. Consolidate Debts:

Explore debt consolidation options, such as transferring high-interest credit card balances to a lower-interest card or taking out a debt consolidation loan. Consolidation can simplify your payments and potentially lower your overall interest rates.

8. Avoid New Debt:

While repaying existing debts, commit to not taking on new debt. Resist the temptation to use credit cards for non-essential purchases, and focus on building a debt-free future.

9. Track Your Progress:

Keep track of your debt repayment progress regularly. Celebrate each milestone achieved, and use your progress as motivation to stay on track.

10. Seek Professional Advice if Needed:

If you're feeling overwhelmed or struggling to manage your debts, consider seeking advice from a financial counselor or debt management professional. They can provide personalized guidance to help you overcome challenges and achieve your debt-free goals.

Remember, building a debt repayment strategy requires discipline and dedication, but the rewards of financial freedom and reduced stress are well worth the effort. Stay committed to your plan, and with each payment, you'll be one step closer to a debt-free future.

***

Chapter 2 has laid the foundation for your financial journey by assessing your current situation and creating a solid financial plan. With a clear understanding of your financial standing and a strategic roadmap, you are now ready to move forward with confidence.

In the next chapter, "Crafting Your Financial Roadmap," we'll explore budgeting, saving, investing, and other essential components that will propel you towards financial success.

Let's continue this empowering journey together towards lasting financial freedom!

Remember,

"Forget the glass ceiling.

Build a glass empire."

Ann B

CHAPTER 3

CRAFTING YOUR FINANCIAL ROADMAP

Welcome to Chapter 3 of "Mapping Your Financial Future: Setting Clear Financial Goals." In this transformative chapter, we'll delve into the essential components that form the foundation of your financial success. As we explore budgeting, saving, investing, and other crucial elements, we'll equip you with the knowledge and strategies to build a powerful financial roadmap that leads you towards lasting financial freedom.

Section 1
Mastering the Art of Budgeting

Budgeting is the cornerstone of a solid financial plan. In this section, we'll guide you through the process of creating a realistic and practical budget that aligns with your financial goals. You'll learn how to track your income and expenses, identify areas for improvement, and make informed financial decisions that optimize your resources.
Creating a realistic and practical budget is an empowering process that aligns your financial decisions with your dreams and aspirations.

Let's embark on this journey together, as we guide you through the steps of crafting a budget that brings you closer to your financial goals.

Step 1: Set Clear Financial Goals

Before diving into the budgeting process, it's essential to have a clear vision of your financial goals. *What do you aspire to achieve in the short, medium, and long term?* Whether it's building an emergency fund, saving for a dream vacation, or investing for retirement, your goals will serve as the guiding stars of your budget.

Step 2: Assess Your Current Financial

Situation Understanding your current financial standing is the foundation of creating an effective budget. Take an honest look at your income, expenses, debts, and savings. This assessment will reveal valuable insights into your spending habits and areas where adjustments may be necessary.

Step 3: Categorize Your Expenses

Break down your expenses into categories such as housing, transportation, groceries, entertainment, and debt payments. This categorization will provide clarity on where your money is going and help you identify potential areas for saving.

Step 4: Differentiate Between Needs and Wants

Distinguish between essential needs and discretionary wants. While some expenses are necessary for daily living, others may be optional. Being mindful of your spending habits will enable you to prioritize what truly matters and allocate resources accordingly.

Step 5: Create a Realistic Budget

With a clear understanding of your financial goals, current situation, and spending patterns, it's time to create your budget. Aim for a realistic budget that aligns with your income and enables you to save and invest for your future. Be flexible and open to adjustments as you fine-tune your budget over time.

Step 6: Track Your Progress

Regularly Monitoring your budget regularly is crucial to staying on track with your financial goals. Use budgeting tools, apps, or spreadsheets to track your income and expenses. This practice will help you identify any deviations and make necessary corrections to ensure you're moving towards your financial aspirations.

Step 7: Make Informed Financial Decisions

As you navigate through your budgeting journey, embrace the empowerment of making informed financial decisions. Each expense becomes a deliberate choice that brings you closer to the life you desire. Remember, budgeting is not about restriction; it's about making choices that align with your priorities.

Step 8: Celebrate Your Victories

Recognize and celebrate your budgeting victories, no matter how small they may seem. Every step towards financial alignment is a step closer to your dreams. Reward yourself for staying committed to your budget and progress.

Creating a realistic and practical budget is a powerful tool that aligns your financial choices with your aspirations. As you embrace this process, you'll gain a newfound sense of control over your financial destiny. Let your budget be a reflection of your values and the life you envision. With each budgeting decision, you're crafting a brighter and more prosperous future. Keep your focus on your goals and dreams, and together, we'll unlock the extraordinary potential within you.

Now we delve into the art of tracking your income and expenses, an essential skill that will empower you to make informed and strategic financial decisions.

Let's embark on this journey together as we explore the power of financial awareness and its impact on your path to prosperity.

Step 1: Embrace Financial Awareness

The first step towards optimizing your financial resources is to embrace financial awareness. This means being mindful of your income sources and how you allocate your hard-earned money. By becoming financially aware, you gain valuable insights into your spending habits and identify areas where adjustments may be needed.

Step 2: Track Your Income

Tracking your income is the foundation of financial awareness. Keep a record of your earnings, including salaries, bonuses, dividends, or any additional income sources. This practice will give you a clear picture of your cash inflows and enable you to plan your budget effectively.

Step 3: Categorize Your Expenses

Organize your expenses into categories, such as housing, utilities, transportation, food, entertainment, and savings. Categorization allows you to see how much you spend in each area, making it easier to identify potential areas for improvement.

Step 4: Monitor Your Spending

Regularly monitor your spending to ensure it aligns with your financial goals. Stay vigilant about discretionary expenses and be mindful of impulsive purchases. Tracking your spending habits will help you identify patterns and make conscious choices.

Step 5: Identify Areas for Improvement

Through financial tracking, you'll be able to pinpoint areas where you can optimize your resources. Are there expenses you can reduce or eliminate? Can you redirect some funds towards savings or investments? Identifying areas for improvement is a powerful step towards financial empowerment.

Step 6: Make Informed Financial Decisions

Armed with financial awareness, you'll make informed financial decisions that align with your goals and values. Each expense becomes a deliberate choice, and each investment is a step towards securing your financial future. Embrace the confidence that comes with taking charge of your finances.

Step 7: Create a Budget That Works for You

With a clear understanding of your income and expenses, create a budget that suits your lifestyle and aspirations. A well-structured budget will enable you to live within your means, save for the future, and achieve your financial objectives.

Step 8: Celebrate Your Financial Progress

As you implement these tracking and decision-making strategies, celebrate your financial progress, no matter how small. Each positive step you take towards financial awareness is a victory. Acknowledge your efforts and use them as motivation to continue your journey towards prosperity.

Tracking your income and expenses is a transformative practice that empowers you to make the most of your financial resources. By becoming financially aware and making informed decisions, you pave the way for a brighter and more prosperous future. Embrace the power of financial tracking, and together, we'll unlock the extraordinary potential within you.

Section 2

The Art of Saving and Investing

Welcome to Section 2: The Art of Saving and Investing. In this part, we'll embark on a transformative journey into the world of financial growth and security. Saving and investing are not just activities; they are powerful tools that will pave the way for building wealth and securing your financial future.

Step 1: Building Your Emergency Fund

Your financial journey begins with the establishment of a robust emergency fund. We'll guide you through the process of setting aside funds for unexpected expenses, creating a safety net that offers peace of mind during challenging times. Learn how to determine the ideal size of your emergency fund and the best strategies to grow it over time.

Secure Your Future: *The Roadmap to Building Your Emergency Fund* exercise.

Life is full of unexpected twists, and having a well-funded emergency fund is your key to weathering any storm that comes your way.Throughout this guided exercise, you'll embark on a transformative journey, learning how to set aside funds for unexpected expenses and take control of your financial well-being. We'll help you determine the ideal size of your emergency fund based on your unique circumstances and unveil the best strategies to grow it over time, ensuring it becomes a reliable shield against financial uncertainties.No longer will you feel vulnerable to unexpected setbacks. Instead, you'll be empowered to build a brighter, more secure future with confidence and determination. So let's dive in and start crafting your financial safety net, one step at a time. Remember, the first step to financial freedom is securing your foundation.

Exercise: Building Your Emergency Fund

1/ Assess Your Current Financial

Situation Start by taking a comprehensive look at your finances. Calculate your monthly income and expenses, including fixed costs like rent or mortgage payments, utility bills, groceries, and discretionary spending. Understanding your cash flow will help you determine how much you can realistically set aside for your emergency fund.

2/ Determine Your Ideal Emergency Fund Size

A common guideline is to have enough funds to cover three to six months' worth of living expenses. However, your ideal emergency fund size may vary based on your individual circumstances. Consider factors such as job stability, family size, and any potential sources of additional income.

3/ Set Clear Savings Goals

Based on your assessment in Step 1 and your ideal emergency fund size from Step 2, set clear and achievable savings goals. Determine how much you need to save each month to reach your target emergency fund size within a reasonable timeframe.

4/ Create a Dedicated Emergency Fund Account

Establish a separate savings account exclusively for your emergency fund. This will help you track your progress and avoid the temptation to dip into these funds for non-emergencies.

5/ Automate Your Savings

Make saving for your emergency fund a seamless process by setting up automatic transfers from your primary checking account to your dedicated emergency fund account. Automating your savings ensures consistency and eliminates the risk of forgetting to contribute regularly.

6/ Prioritize Debt Repayment

If you have outstanding debts, consider prioritizing debt repayment while simultaneously building your emergency fund. Striking a balance between saving and debt repayment will put you on a path towards financial security.

7/ Explore Additional Income Streams

Increase your emergency fund savings by exploring additional income streams. Consider taking on a part-time job, freelancing, or selling unused items to generate extra cash for your fund.

8/ Revise and Adjust as Needed

Life circumstances change, and so may your financial goals. Periodically review and adjust your emergency fund size based on any changes in your income, expenses, or family situation.

9/ Stay Committed and Stay Calm

Building an emergency fund takes time and discipline. Stay committed to your savings goals and remain patient during the process. Remember that each contribution brings you closer to the peace of mind that comes with having a robust safety net.

10/ Celebrate Milestones

Celebrate each milestone achieved in your emergency fund journey. Whether it's reaching a certain percentage of your goal or achieving your target fund size, acknowledge your progress and use it as motivation to keep going.

Conclusion

By diligently following these steps and consistently contributing to your emergency fund, you'll create a safety net that offers peace of mind during challenging times. Building your emergency fund is a powerful step towards financial security, ensuring you are well-prepared to handle unexpected expenses and emergencies that may arise.

Step 2: Targeted Savings for Your Goals

Unlock the potential of targeted savings as we explore the art of saving for specific financial goals. Whether you're dreaming of a dream vacation, a down payment for a new home, or funding your entrepreneurial venture, we'll show you how to set clear goals and create dedicated savings plans to achieve them.

Creating Targeted Savings Accounts for Your Financial Goals.

1/ Identifying Your Financial Goals

Write Down Your Goals: Take a moment to identify your specific financial goals. Whether it's a dream vacation, buying a new car, or saving for a down payment on a house, write down each goal and its estimated amount.

Categorize Your Goals: Group your financial goals into short-term, medium-term, and long-term categories. This will help you prioritize your savings and allocate resources effectively.

Set Timelines: Assign a timeline to each goal and determine when you want to achieve them. Having specific timelines will keep you motivated and focused on your objectives.

2/ Creating Individual Savings Accounts

Calculate Monthly Savings: Based on the timeline and total amount needed for each goal, calculate the monthly savings required. Divide the total amount by the number of months you have to save.

Open Separate Savings Accounts: Open dedicated savings accounts for each of your targeted financial goals. Consider naming each account after the specific goal it represents.

3/ Implementing Your Savings Plan

Automate Your Savings: Set up automatic transfers from your main account to each targeted savings account. This ensures consistent progress towards your goals.

Monitor and Adjust: Regularly review your progress towards each financial goal. Assess if you're on track and adjust your savings strategy if needed.

4/ Celebrating Your Milestones

Celebrate Your Achievements: As you reach each financial goal, celebrate your milestones and accomplishments. Treat yourself to something special or acknowledge the progress you've made.

Remember, setting up targeted savings accounts for specific financial goals empowers you to achieve your objectives and provides a sense of financial security. Stay disciplined and focused on your journey to financial success!

Step 3: Understanding the World of Investing

Delve into the world of investing as we demystify the complexities and empower you with valuable insights. Understand various investment options, from stocks and bonds to mutual funds and real estate. Learn how to assess your risk tolerance and choose investments that align with your financial goals.

Assessing Your Risk Tolerance: Finding the Perfect Investment Fit

In the world of finance, one size does not fit all. Just as we have unique aspirations and financial goals, our tolerance for risk varies as well. Understanding your risk tolerance is essential for making informed investment decisions that align with your financial objectives.

1/ Reflect on Your Risk Comfort Level

Take a moment to reflect on your comfort level with investment risk. Are you someone who prefers safe and stable investments, even if they offer lower returns, or are you willing to take on higher risks in pursuit of potentially higher rewards? Your risk comfort level will serve as the foundation for crafting an investment strategy tailored to your preferences.

2/ Define Your Investment Goals

Clarify your investment goals and time horizon. Are you investing for short-term gains, such as purchasing a new car or going on a dream vacation, or are you focused on long-term objectives, such as funding your retirement or building wealth for future generations? Understanding your investment goals will help you choose investments that are in line with your financial vision.

3/ Assess Your Financial Situation

Consider your current financial situation, including your income, expenses, and existing investments. Evaluate how much disposable income you have to allocate towards investments and how much risk you can comfortably take without jeopardizing your financial stability.

4/ Diversification

The Key to Balanced Risk Diversification is a powerful strategy for managing risk in your investment portfolio. By spreading your investments across different asset classes, industries, and regions, you reduce the impact of any single investment on your overall portfolio. This diversification helps maintain a balanced risk exposure.

5/ Seek Professional Guidance

If you find assessing your risk tolerance challenging or are unsure about making investment decisions, seek guidance from a financial advisor. A qualified professional can help you evaluate your risk tolerance, explore investment options, and create a personalized investment strategy that aligns with your unique financial situation and goals.

6/ Regularly Reassess Your Risk Tolerance

As life evolves, so do our risk preferences. It's essential to reassess your risk tolerance regularly, especially during significant life events such as marriage, the birth of a child, or retirement. Stay attuned to any changes in your financial circumstances or goals and adjust your investment strategy accordingly.

Conclusion: Finding the perfect investment fit involves a careful balance between your risk comfort level, investment goals, and financial situation. By taking the time to assess your risk tolerance and aligning your investments with your financial vision, you'll be better equipped to navigate the ever-changing landscape of the financial markets and move confidently towards achieving your financial dreams.

Step 4: Building a Diversified Investment Portfolio

Unlock the secret to successful investing through the art of building a diversified investment portfolio. We'll guide you in spreading your investments across various asset classes to minimize risk and maximize potential returns. Discover the power of diversification as you build a strong foundation for your financial future.

Step 5: Navigating Market Volatility

While investing offers tremendous growth potential, it's essential to navigate the ever-changing landscape of market volatility. Learn how to remain calm during market fluctuations, make rational decisions, and stay committed to your long-term financial goals.

Staying Calm in Market Fluctuations: Building Resilience for Long-Term Financial Success Market fluctuations are a natural part of investing, but they can sometimes lead to emotional decisions that may not align with your long-term financial goals. This exercise will help you build resilience and make rational choices during market ups and downs.

1/ Understanding Market Fluctuations

Educate Yourself: Learn about the nature of market fluctuations and how they are a normal part of the investing process. Understand that markets go through cycles and that short-term fluctuations are not indicative of long-term performance.

Identify Your Risk Tolerance: Assess your risk tolerance and understand how comfortable you are with market volatility. This self-awareness will guide you in making investment decisions that align with your emotional and financial comfort levels.

2/ Creating a Resilience Strategy

- Develop an Investment Plan: Work with a financial advisor to create a well-diversified investment plan that aligns with your long-term financial goals. A balanced portfolio can help mitigate the impact of market fluctuations.

- Set Clear Objectives: Define your long-term financial goals and set clear objectives for your investments. Having a purpose-driven approach will keep you focused during uncertain times.

- Establish an Emergency Fund: Build an emergency fund that covers three to six months' worth of living expenses. Having this safety net will provide peace of mind during challenging market conditions.

3/ Cultivating Emotional Resilience

- Practice Mindfulness:

Incorporate mindfulness techniques into your daily routine to stay present and calm during market fluctuations. Meditation, deep breathing, and grounding exercises can help you maintain emotional balance.

- Avoid Emotional Decision-Making:

When the market is volatile, avoid making impulsive decisions based on fear or greed.

Refer back to your investment plan and long-term objectives before making any changes.

4/ Staying Committed to Your Goals

- Focus on the Long Term: Remind yourself that investing is a journey, and short-term fluctuations are just part of the process. Stay committed to your long-term financial goals, and avoid getting derailed by temporary market movements.

- Regularly Review Your Plan: Periodically review your investment plan with your financial advisor. Discuss any changes in your life circumstances or financial goals, and make adjustments as needed.

5/ Celebrating Your Financial Resilience

- Acknowledge Your Progress: Celebrate your ability to remain calm and rational during market fluctuations. Recognize the resilience you've built and the progress you've made towards your long-term financial success.

- Remember, staying calm during market fluctuations and making rational decisions are essential for achieving your long-term financial goals. By building emotional resilience and staying committed to your investment plan, you'll navigate market ups and downs with confidence and poise.

Step 6: Taking Advantage of Tax-Efficient Strategies

Explore tax-efficient strategies that can help you keep more of your hard-earned money. We'll guide you through tax-advantaged accounts and other tactics to optimize your tax situation and bolster your savings and investment growth.

Unlocking Tax-Smart Strategies for Financial Growth

Navigating the complexities of taxes can seem like a daunting task, but fear not – we're here to guide you through tax-advantaged accounts and other tactics that will optimize your tax situation and boost your savings and investment growth.

Phase 1: Understanding Tax-Advantaged Accounts

- Explore Retirement Accounts: Learn about the various tax-advantaged retirement accounts, such as 401(k)s, IRAs, and Roth IRAs. Understand how contributing to these accounts can provide tax benefits while building a secure financial future.

- Maximize Employer Benefits: If your employer offers a retirement savings plan with matching contributions, take full advantage of this opportunity. It's essentially free money that can supercharge your retirement savings.

Phase 2: Optimizing Tax Efficiency

- Tax-Loss Harvesting: Discover the concept of tax-loss harvesting, where you strategically sell losing investments to offset capital gains and potentially reduce your tax liability.

- Dividend and Capital Gain Strategies: Understand how dividends and capital gains are taxed differently and explore strategies to minimize their impact on your overall tax situation.

Phase 3: Harnessing Tax Deductions and Credits

- Deduction Opportunities: Familiarize yourself with common tax deductions that you may be eligible for, such as mortgage interest, student loan interest, and charitable contributions.

- Tax Credits: Learn about valuable tax credits that can directly reduce your tax bill, such as the Child Tax Credit, Earned Income Tax Credit, and Education Credits.

Phase 4: Leveraging Health Savings Accounts (HSAs)

- HSA Benefits: Discover the powerful advantages of Health Savings Accounts (HSAs) for those with high-deductible health insurance plans. HSAs offer triple tax benefits and can be an excellent tool for managing healthcare expenses in retirement.

Phase 5: Staying Informed and Adaptable

- Stay Updated on Tax Laws: Be aware of changes in tax laws and regulations that may impact your financial decisions. Staying informed will help you make timely and informed choices.

- Consult with Tax Professionals: Consider seeking advice from tax professionals who can provide personalized guidance based on your unique financial situation. Their expertise can help you make the most of tax-saving opportunities.

Phase 6: Celebrating Financial Freedom

- Embrace Your Tax-Smart Financial

Strategy: Celebrate your newfound knowledge and embrace the confidence that comes with optimizing your tax situation. Your tax-smart approach will accelerate your savings and investment growth, bringing you closer to financial freedom.

Remember, tax-smart strategies are essential for maximizing your financial growth and preserving more of your hard-earned money. By implementing these tactics and staying informed, you'll pave the way to a brighter financial future.

Step 7: Embracing the Power of Compounding

Witness the magic of compounding as we demonstrate how consistent saving and investing can lead to exponential growth over time. Embrace the power of time and patience as you let your investments work for you and multiply your wealth.

As we move forward in this book, remember that each step you take towards financial empowerment is a step towards lasting prosperity. Together, let's embrace the art of saving and investing and unlock the extraordinary potential within you.

Conclusion

Chapter 3 has equipped you with essential financial tools and strategies for crafting your financial roadmap. By mastering the art of budgeting, saving, and investing, you have taken significant steps towards achieving lasting financial freedom.

In the next chapter, "Overcoming Challenges and Staying Focused," we'll address common setbacks and provide you with powerful strategies to stay motivated during challenging times. Let's continue this transformative journey together and unlock the extraordinary potential that lies within you.

CHAPTER 4

ACHIEVING FINANCIAL CONFIDENCE

&

OVERCOMING CHALLENGES AND STAYING FOCUSED

In this pivotal chapter, we will delve into the core essence of achieving financial confidence. Life is full of uncertainties, and the journey to financial success is no exception. But fear not, as we equip you with the tools to overcome challenges and stay laser-focused on your path to prosperity. Let's fortify your resilience, conquer obstacles, and unleash your unwavering determination.

Section 1

Building unshakeable resilience

Resilience is your superpower in the face of adversity. Discover the art of embracing challenges as stepping stones to growth and learning. We'll explore real-life stories of individuals who have triumphed over financial setbacks, showing you that resilience is not just a trait but a skill that can be cultivated.

In the face of life's challenges and financial uncertainties, resilience becomes your superpower – the key to overcoming obstacles and forging ahead with unwavering determination. Embracing resilience means viewing challenges not as roadblocks but as opportunities for growth and learning. It's about recognizing that setbacks are an integral part of any journey to success, and each obstacle you encounter is a stepping stone towards a brighter future.

Real-life stories of individuals who have triumphed over financial setbacks will inspire and motivate you. These stories exemplify the power of resilience and showcase how ordinary people, like you, have transformed adversity into triumph. You'll see that resilience is not an innate trait reserved for the few but a skill that can be cultivated and nurtured.

Embracing resilience involves adopting a mindset that embraces change, embraces uncertainty, and embraces the belief that you have the inner strength to navigate through turbulent times. It means acknowledging that setbacks and failures are not permanent, but temporary detours on your path to success. With resilience, you can bounce back from financial challenges, adapt to changing circumstances, and emerge stronger and more determined than ever.

As we explore the art of embracing resilience, you'll gain practical strategies for building your resilience muscle. You'll learn how to shift your perspective, reframe challenges as opportunities, and develop emotional intelligence to navigate through financial ups and downs with grace.

Remember, resilience is not about avoiding difficulties or pretending that everything is perfect. It's about acknowledging the challenges, facing them head-on, and using them as catalysts for growth and personal development. By embracing resilience, you'll have the power to persevere, stay focused on your financial goals, and confidently steer your financial journey towards lasting success.Let the stories of resilience from others inspire you and serve as a reminder that you, too, have the strength to embrace challenges, transform setbacks into stepping stones, and create a future filled with financial empowerment and prosperity.

The journey may not always be smooth, but with resilience as your guiding force, you'll have the courage and determination to conquer any obstacle that comes your way.

Real-Life Story:

Leila's Journey to Financial Triumph

Meet Leila, a determined and resilient woman who faced significant financial setbacks early in her career. After graduating from college, she landed a job in a promising startup but

when the company faced financial difficulties and had to lay off employees.

Initially devastated by the sudden job loss, Leila took some time to reflect on her situation. Instead of succumbing to despair, she decided to view this setback as an opportunity to explore new possibilities. She enrolled in online courses to expand her skills, attended networking events to connect with potential employers, and started freelancing to generate income while seeking a new full-time position.

Though the journey was challenging, Leila remained committed to her financial goals and maintained a positive outlook. Her resilience paid off when she secured a new position with a growing company that valued her expertise and offered better career prospects.

Throughout her journey, Leila learned that resilience is not just an inherent trait but a skill that can be cultivated through practice and self-belief. She discovered the power of adaptability, resourcefulness, and the importance of maintaining a strong support system during tough times.

Exercice

CULTIVATING RESILIENCE THROUGH SELF-REFLECTION

Embracing resilience starts with understanding your strengths and areas for growth. Take some time for self-reflection and answer the following questions:

1. What are some challenging financial situations or setbacks you have faced in the past, and how did you overcome them? Reflect on the strategies you employed and the lessons you learned.

2. Identify the key strengths and qualities you demonstrated during those

challenging times. Were you persistent, resourceful, or optimistic? Recognize and celebrate these qualities as part of your resilience.

3. Consider any moments when you may have felt overwhelmed or discouraged. What could you have done differently to maintain a more positive outlook and keep moving forward?

4. Think about individuals who have inspired you with their resilience in the face of financial setbacks. What specific traits or actions did they exhibit that you can incorporate into your own approach?

5. How can you apply the lessons from your past experiences and the examples of resilient individuals to your current financial situation? Identify actionable steps to strengthen your resilience and navigate through future challenges.

Remember, resilience is not about being invincible or never experiencing difficulties. It's about developing the capacity to bounce back, grow, and thrive in the face of adversity. By embracing the power of resilience, you can cultivate a mindset that empowers you to turn setbacks into opportunities and create a brighter financial future.

- Mastering Emotional Intelligence -

Emotional intelligence is a critical skill when navigating financial ups and downs. Learn how to regulate your emotions, make rational decisions during market fluctuations, and build unwavering confidence in your financial choices.

Mastering Emotional Intelligence: Navigating Financial Ups and Downs with Confidence

In the ever-changing landscape of finance, emotional intelligence is a crucial skill that sets apart successful individuals from those who struggle to make sound financial decisions. Emotional intelligence, often referred to as EQ, encompasses the ability to understand and manage emotions effectively, both in ourselves and in others. When it comes to managing finances, EQ plays a central role in our decision-making, risk tolerance, and overall financial well-being.

Regulating Your Emotions: The Key to Financial Stability

Financial markets are inherently volatile, and the emotions of fear and greed can easily sway our judgment. Mastering emotional intelligence allows us to regulate these emotions, preventing rash decisions that may lead to unfavorable outcomes.

By understanding the impact of emotions on our financial choices, we can cultivate a sense of calm and rationality even during market turbulence.

Recognizing Emotional Triggers: Building Self-Awareness

To navigate financial ups and downs with confidence, it is essential to recognize our emotional triggers. When we encounter unexpected financial events or market fluctuations, certain emotions may arise, such as anxiety, excitement, or even panic. By building self-awareness, we can identify these triggers and take a step back to assess the situation with clarity and objectivity.

Making Rational Financial Decisions: The Role of EQ

Emotional intelligence enables us to make rational financial decisions, free from the influence of impulsive emotions. Instead of being driven solely by fear or greed, we can weigh the pros and cons, consider long-term objectives, and make choices aligned with our financial goals.

Building Unwavering Confidence: Trusting Your Financial Choices

Confidence in our financial decisions is an outcome of emotional intelligence. As we develop the ability to manage emotions and make rational choices, we naturally build trust in our judgment and financial acumen. This unwavering confidence empowers us to stay committed to our financial plans, even during challenging times.

Action Steps: Cultivating Emotional Intelligence in Financial Decision-Making

1. Reflect on Past Financial Decisions:Take some time to think about past financial decisions and the emotions that influenced them. Identify any patterns or tendencies that may have led to either positive or negative outcomes.

2. Practice Mindfulness: Incorporate mindfulness practices into your daily routine. Meditation, deep breathing exercises, or journaling can help you become more in tune with your emotions and cultivate a sense of inner calm.

3. Seek Perspective: When faced with a financial decision, seek input from trusted advisors or friends who can provide a fresh perspective. Sometimes, an outside viewpoint can help us see things more clearly and objectively.

4. Set Clear Financial Goals: Define your long-term financial goals and set clear objectives for achieving them. When you have a well-defined plan, it becomes easier to stay focused and make decisions that align with your vision.

5. Monitor Your Emotional Responses: Pay attention to your emotional responses during financial conversations or when monitoring market fluctuations. Practice acknowledging these emotions without immediately reacting to them. Take a moment to pause and consider the best course of action.

In conclusion, emotional intelligence is a powerful tool that enables us to navigate financial ups and downs with confidence and resilience. By mastering EQ, we can regulate our emotions, make rational decisions, and build the unwavering confidence needed to achieve our financial aspirations. Embrace the power of emotional intelligence and unlock the potential to create a secure and prosperous financial future.

- Overcoming Financial Obstacles -

Life is unpredictable, and financial obstacles are inevitable. In this section, I'll equip you with the tools to overcome common financial challenges and maintain your financial well-being. Whether it's tackling debt, managing unexpected expenses, or navigating major life transitions, I'll guide you in finding effective solutions and staying on track with your financial goals.

From creating a contingency plan to building a flexible budget, you'll develop the resilience and adaptability to overcome any financial hurdles that come your way. I'll also address the psychological aspects of money and how to maintain a positive and constructive mindset when facing financial challenges.

Identify and Tackle Debt

Debt can feel overwhelming, but with a strategic approach, you can conquer it. Start by listing all your debts, including credit card balances, loans, and other obligations. Calculate the interest rates and prioritize paying off higher-interest debts first. Create a debt repayment plan, allocating extra funds to the highest interest debt while making minimum payments on others. As you pay off one debt, roll over the payments to the next, creating a snowball effect that accelerates your debt reduction journey.

Prepare for Unexpected Expenses

Life's surprises often come with unexpected costs. Establishing an emergency fund is essential to weathering these financial storms. Aim to save three to six months worth of living expenses in a separate account. This fund acts as a safety net, allowing you to cover unforeseen expenses without derailing your financial goals. Regularly contribute to your emergency fund, and only use it for genuine emergencies, such as medical bills or urgent home repairs.

Navigate Major Life Transitions

Major life events, such as marriage, parenthood, or job changes, can have a significant impact on your finances. Prepare for these transitions by reviewing your financial plan and making necessary adjustments. If your income changes, revisit your budget and ensure it aligns with your new financial reality. Update your insurance coverage, beneficiaries, and estate planning documents to reflect your current circumstances. By proactively planning for life changes, you'll be better equipped to manage their financial implications.

Create a Flexible Budget

A budget is a powerful tool that provides financial clarity and control. Develop a flexible budget that accounts for both essential expenses and discretionary spending. Allocate a portion of your income to savings and investments, and set aside funds for fun and leisure. Regularly review and adjust your budget based on changing circumstances. A flexible budget empowers you to make informed spending decisions while remaining adaptable to unexpected changes.

EXERCISE:
OVERCOMING FINANCIAL OBSTACLES

1. Debt Assessment: List all your current debts, their interest rates, and minimum payments. Calculate the total amount of debt you owe. Reflect on how this debt affects your financial well-being and set a goal to pay it off systematically.

2. Emergency Fund Goal: Determine the ideal amount for your emergency fund based on your monthly expenses. Calculate how much you need to save to reach that goal. Begin contributing regularly to your emergency fund, and track your progress over time.

3. Life Transition Planning: Consider potential major life transitions you may experience in the future. How might these

transitions impact your finances? Create a plan for each scenario, outlining the steps you would take to ensure financial stability.

4. Budget Redesign: Review your current budget and identify areas where you can cut back or reallocate funds to prioritize your financial goals. Revise your budget

to create more room for savings and investments while still enjoying the things that bring you joy.

Remember, financial obstacles are opportunities for growth and learning. By proactively addressing challenges and developing effective strategies, you can maintain your financial well-being and stay on course to achieve your long-term goals.

Contingency Plan for Building a Flexible Budget:

In the ever-changing landscape of personal finance, being prepared for the unexpected is a cornerstone of financial success. Our Contingency Plan for Building a Flexible Budget equips you with a strategic approach to handle unforeseen expenses while staying firmly on the path towards your financial goals.

Life's surprises can manifest as medical emergencies, sudden repairs, or unexpected job transitions. Our comprehensive plan ensures you're not only ready for these challenges but also have the financial capacity to weather them without compromising your overall financial stability.

By proactively integrating contingency strategies into your budget, you'll forge a safety net that safeguards your financial well-being and empowers you to navigate the unpredictable with confidence. Let's dive into the details of this plan and discover how it can fortify your financial foundation.

CONTINGENCY PLAN:
Building a Flexible Budget for Unforeseen Expenses

1. Identify Potential Risks: Begin by identifying potential financial risks or unexpected expenses that could impact your budget. These could include medical emergencies, car repairs, home maintenance, job loss, or any other significant unexpected costs.

2. Emergency Fund Allocation: Allocate a specific portion of your budget to your emergency fund. This fund serves as a safety net to cover unforeseen expenses

without disrupting your overall financial plan. Aim to gradually build an emergency fund equivalent to 3 to 6 months' worth of living expenses.

3. Create a "Miscellaneous" Category: In your budget, include a "Miscellaneous" or "Unforeseen Expenses" category. Allocate a small percentage of your income to this category. This provides flexibility to address unexpected costs without affecting other budgeted areas.

4. Prioritize Savings: Treat savings as a non-negotiable expense in your budget. Designate a portion of your income for savings goals such as short-term (vacations, electronics) and long-term (retirement, education) goals. This way, you'll have funds set aside for future expenses.

5. Review and Adjust Monthly: Regularly review your budget, especially the contingency components. If you dip into your emergency fund or the miscellaneous category, adjust your budget for the following months to replenish these funds.

6. Scale Down Discretionary Spending: When unexpected expenses arise, consider temporarily scaling down discretionary spending. This could mean

cutting back on entertainment, dining out, or non-essential purchases until your budget is back on track.

7. Use Windfalls Wisely: If you receive unexpected windfalls like bonuses, tax refunds, or gifts, allocate a portion to your emergency fund or savings categories. This boosts your contingency fund and ensures you're prepared for future surprises.

8. Explore Alternative Income Streams: Building flexibility into your budget might involve exploring side gigs or freelance opportunities. The extra income can serve as a cushion for unexpected expenses and allow you to stay on track with your financial goals.

9. Stay Adaptable: Life is dynamic, and circumstances change. A flexible budget requires adaptability. If your financial situation changes (e.g., income increase, decrease, new expenses), adjust your budget categories to accommodate the changes.

10. Reevaluate Regularly: Periodically assess the effectiveness of your contingency plan.

Are your emergency fund and miscellaneous categories adequately funded?

Have you encountered unexpected expenses that your budget didn't cover?

Make adjustments as needed.

By integrating these contingency strategies into your budget, you'll create a safety net that cushions the impact of unforeseen expenses. This proactive approach to budgeting ensures that you have the financial flexibility to navigate unexpected challenges while staying on track toward your long-term financial goals.

Now let's have a look at the psychology of money and how to maintain a positive and constructive mindset in the face of financial challenges.

Money isn't just about numbers; it has powerful psychological implications that can impact our attitudes, behaviors and overall well-being. In this section, we'll dive into the fascinating field of financial psychology, exploring how our beliefs, emotions, and thought patterns influence our financial decisions.

• Understanding your financial mindset

Your mindset about money shapes your financial reality. We'll guide you through uncovering your deep-rooted beliefs about money - whether they stem from childhood, cultural influences, or personal experiences. By clarifying your mindset when it comes to money, you'll be better equipped to make conscious financial choices that align with your goals.

Example: Let's say you grew up thinking that money is scarce and hard to come by. This mindset can lead you to make overly cautious financial decisions, to miss out on potential opportunities. By recognizing and reshaping this belief, you can open yourself up to new possibilities and abundance.

- Cultivate a positive financial mindset:

Maintaining a positive financial mindset is essential, especially during tough times. We will provide practical techniques for moving from a mindset of scarcity to a mindset of abundance and empowerment. By focusing on gratitude, affirmations, and visualization, you will create a mental environment conducive to financial success.

Example: Instead of dwelling on financial setbacks, practice gratitude for what you've accomplished so far. Regularly affirm your financial goals and look to the future with confidence. This positive mindset can boost your motivation and resilience, helping you stay on track even in the face of obstacles.

- Overcome Emotional Spending and Impulse Buying:

Emotional spending is a common behavior rooted in emotions rather than genuine necessity. We will explore strategies to identify the emotional triggers that lead to impulse buying. By developing awareness and adopting healthy coping mechanisms, you can regain control of your spending habits and make wise financial choices.

Example: When you feel stressed, you may notice a tendency to indulge in retail therapy. Instead, channel that energy into healthier alternatives like exercise, meditation, or spending quality time with loved ones. This change not only promotes emotional well-being, but also avoids unnecessary financial strain.

- Managing Financial Stress and Anxiety:

Financial difficulties often lead to stress and anxiety. We will provide you with effective stress management techniques tailored to your financial situation. From hands-on exercises to mindfulness practices, you'll learn how to manage stress while maintaining a clear and focused mindset.

Example: In times of financial uncertainty, practice deep breathing exercises or engage in mindfulness meditation. These techniques can relieve anxiety and improve your decision-making skills, allowing you to approach financial challenges with a calmer demeanor.

By addressing the psychological aspects of money and cultivating a positive financial mindset, you will not only improve your ability to overcome challenges, but you will also create a solid foundation for long-term financial success.

Remember, a healthy money mindset is a powerful tool that can turn your financial journey into one of empowerment and fulfillment.

Amidst the pursuit of financial success, it's essential to celebrate your achievements and acknowledge your progress. In this section, we'll emphasize the importance of recognizing your financial victories, no matter how small they may seem.

By celebrating your accomplishments, you reinforce positive financial behaviors and stay motivated on your financial journey. We'll explore creative ways to reward yourself for reaching milestones and how these celebrations inspire you to keep pushing forward towards your long-term financial goals.

- Celebrating Your Financial Victories

As you journey toward financial success, amid the intricate challenges, there is a fundamental element that often goes unnoticed – the act of celebrating your achievements. This section brings into focus the significance of acknowledging and commemorating your financial victories, irrespective of their scale.

Why Celebrate? Celebrations are more than mere indulgences; they are potent tools that reinforce positive financial behaviors and stoke your motivation. Through celebration, you create a virtuous cycle of encouragement that propels you toward your financial dreams. These moments of revelry act as milestones, enriching your financial voyage and making it more enduring.

Examples of Financial Victories: Financial triumphs manifest in diverse forms, and it's crucial to appreciate them all. It might involve a substantial achievement like significantly reducing your debt, or something more modest like consistently adhering to your budget for a month. Landing a new job, saving a specific amount, or making your first investment all merit recognition.

- The Ripple Effect

Celebrating your financial victories triggers a ripple effect that permeates every facet of your journey. It strengthens the positive behaviors that pave your path to success, generating a sense of accomplishment and contentment. As you mark each milestone, you'll find renewed determination to overcome challenges, propelled by the sense of advancement.

- Ways to Celebrate

Creative avenues for celebration abound, catering to your preferences and lifestyle. You might treat yourself to a favorite meal, embark on a weekend getaway, or indulge in a cherished hobby. Allocate a small portion of your savings to these celebrations, ensuring they harmonize with your overarching financial strategy.

- Inspiration and Momentum:

Celebrations possess a unique ability to kindle inspiration and momentum. They serve as reminders of the strides you've taken and the ground you've covered. This newfound energy evolves into a propelling force, urging you to conquer new heights and address your next set of financial objectives.

- Sustaining Enthusiasm:

The financial journey is a marathon, not a sprint. It meanders through challenges that can occasionally test your resolve. Celebrations inject enthusiasm and excitement into your journey, acting as beacons of light during trying times. They serve as poignant reminders that the path, though winding, is adorned with accomplishments and potential.

In this section, I have not only underscored the importance of celebrating your financial victories but also provided a wealth of insights on how to infuse your expedition with motivation and positivity.

Remember, each milestone, no matter how seemingly trivial, stands as a testament to your commitment and diligence. Embrace these victories wholeheartedly, for they form the foundation stones of your ultimate financial triumph.

Conclusion

Building unshakeable resilience is a journey of self-discovery and growth. In "Achieving Financial Confidence: Overcoming Challenges and Staying Focused," you've learned to embrace resilience, master emotional intelligence, and overcome financial obstacles with grace.

As you continue on your financial path, remember that resilience is not about never falling but rising each time you do. By cultivating emotional intelligence and celebrating your victories, you'll stay committed to your financial goals, even in the face of uncertainty.

Section 2

Staying Focused on Your Financial Goals

Cultivating Consistent Habits for Financial Victory

Consistency lays the foundation for enduring success. In this section, we delve into the transformative concept of the compound effect. It's like planting seeds of financial prosperity that grow into mighty trees over time. Small, intentional financial habits, practiced consistently, lead to remarkable long-term gains.

Imagine saving a modest percentage of your income every month. Over the years, this consistent effort accumulates into a substantial safety net, ready to catch you during unexpected financial storms. Likewise, meticulously tracking your expenses, no matter how insignificant, unveils valuable insights into your spending patterns and areas for improvement.

These seemingly minor actions, when done consistently, can pave the way for monumental changes in your financial landscape. Begin with manageable steps, and as these habits become engrained in your daily routine, watch them flourish into powerful tools for financial empowerment.

The Power of Automating Finances

Enter the world of financial automation, where convenience and strategy intersect. Discover how to orchestrate automatic transfers, bill payments, and contributions to your savings and investment accounts. By weaving automation into your financial fabric, you reduce the chances of oversight and ensure that your financial commitments are met seamlessly.

Embracing automation not only frees your time and mental energy but also acts as a shield against impulsive spending. It enforces a disciplined approach to managing your money, allowing you to allocate resources towards your goals with precision. As your financial affairs hum along smoothly, you'll have the mental space to focus on strategic decisions and enjoy the journey towards your aspirations.

Staying Committed to Your Financial Journey: The path to financial success is a marathon, not a sprint. Maintaining unwavering focus and commitment is paramount. In this segment, we explore techniques to sustain motivation, track progress, and celebrate the milestones that adorn your journey.

Learn the art of crafting a vision board – a visual representation of your financial dreams. Regularly encountering your aspirations in this tangible form fuels your determination and bolsters your focus on your objectives. We also unravel the strength of accountability, revealing how a support system can transform your financial voyage into an engaging and shared experience.

- Learn the Art of Crafting a Vision Board and Embracing Accountability

CRAFTING YOUR FINANCIAL VISION BOARD

Imagine having a powerful tool that brings your financial dreams to life. A vision board is precisely that – a creative and visual representation of your goals. To start, gather magazines, images, and quotes that resonate with your financial aspirations. Arrange them on a board or a digital platform, creating a collage that vividly depicts the life you envision. If your goal is a dream vacation, find images of your desired destination, luxury accommodations, and thrilling activities. If you're aiming for financial independence, include visuals of financial milestones, symbols of freedom, and your desired lifestyle.

Place your vision board in a prominent location where you'll see it daily. Each glance reinforces your commitment, triggers positive emotions, and strengthens your resolve to make financial decisions aligned with your goals. As you witness your dreams materialize before your eyes, your determination to stay on course intensifies, propelling you towards financial success.

Harnessing the Power of Accountability: Accountability is a game-changer on your financial journey. When you share your goals with a trusted friend, family member, or mentor, you invite them to join you on your voyage to success. Regular check-ins and discussions about your progress create a sense of responsibility, motivating you to stay dedicated.

Consider forming a financial accountability group with like-minded individuals who share your aspirations. Meetings can involve sharing updates, discussing challenges, and offering encouragement. This collective support system turns your financial journey into a shared adventure, providing fresh perspectives and creative solutions.

Furthermore, working with a financial advisor amplifies your accountability. A knowledgeable advisor provides expert guidance, helps you stay on track, and holds you to your commitments. They tailor strategies to your unique circumstances, ensuring you make informed decisions and remain accountable to your goals.

Embracing the combination of crafting a vision board and accountability not only empowers your financial voyage but also makes it an inspiring and interactive experience. As you visualize your dreams and share your progress, you create a positive loop of motivation and determination, propelling you towards the financial confidence you seek. Remember, your dreams are worth pursuing, and with the right tools and support, you have the ability to turn them into reality.

- Teaming Up with a Financial Advisor and Embracing a Community of Like-Minded Individuals.

Teaming up with a financial advisor or immersing yourself in a community of like-minded individuals infuses your journey with encouragement and shared wisdom. With the right support, staying committed to your financial path becomes an exciting and gratifying endeavor.

Embarking on a journey towards financial success is undoubtedly a rewarding pursuit, but it doesn't have to be a solitary one. In fact, seeking the right support can exponentially enhance your experience and outcomes. Whether you choose to team up with a seasoned financial advisor or immerse yourself in a community of like-minded individuals, you're opening the doors to a world of encouragement, shared wisdom, and enriched learning.

- Teaming Up with a Financial Advisor

A financial advisor is like a co-pilot on your financial journey. They bring expertise, insight, and a strategic perspective that can guide you through even the most complex financial decisions. Collaborating with a skilled advisor means you're not alone in navigating the intricate landscape of investments, savings, and wealth-building. They tailor strategies to your unique goals, risk tolerance, and financial situation, ensuring every step you take is a calculated and informed one.

Your financial advisor becomes your confidante, your sounding board, and your partner in turning your financial aspirations into reality. Regular consultations provide opportunities to discuss progress, make adjustments, and address any concerns, all while staying firmly aligned with your overarching objectives. With a financial advisor by your side, you're empowered with knowledge, confidence, and a clear roadmap towards financial success.

- Embracing a Community of Like-Minded Individuals

The power of community cannot be understated, especially when it comes to your financial journey. Surrounding yourself with individuals who share your ambitions, values, and determination creates a dynamic and motivating environment. In a community of like-minded individuals, you're part of a collective force that propels each other forward, celebrating victories and offering support during challenges.

Engaging in group discussions, attending workshops, and participating in networking events within your financial community exposes you to diverse perspectives and innovative strategies. You'll gain insights from those who have walked similar paths, learn from their experiences, and find inspiration in their successes. The sense of camaraderie and mutual encouragement infuses your financial journey with positivity, making every milestone a shared celebration.

Together, teaming up with a financial advisor or immersing yourself in a community of like-minded individuals transforms your commitment to your financial path into an exciting and gratifying endeavor. You'll draw strength from their guidance, harness the power of collective wisdom, and confidently stride towards your financial goals. With the right support, your journey becomes more than a quest for financial success – it becomes a transformative and empowering life experience.

As you tread further on your financial odyssey, remember that resilience fortifies your spirit, consistency propels enduring change, and automation streamlines your path. Together, we're shaping a legacy of financial abundance and empowerment.

Your next steps beckon – prepare to explore advanced financial strategies, unveil the art of strategic investments, and embrace wealth-building tactics. Brace yourself to elevate your financial wisdom and unlock the full spectrum of your financial brilliance.

Let's start first with a powerful empowerment exercise for ambitious businesswomen that I'm thrilled to share with you in this book.

In the journey towards achieving ambitious business goals, empowerment and personal growth play a central role. This carefully curated exercise is designed to provide business-savvy women with the tools and strategies to realize their full potential, overcome challenges, and create lasting impact in the business world.

Through this exercise, you will embark on a transformative exploration of your strengths, aspirations, and the unique qualities that set you apart as a self-directed business leader.

We'll dive into actionable steps and insights that will empower you to take charge of your career journey, make informed decisions, and navigate the dynamic business landscape with confidence.

As you engage in this exercise, remember that empowerment is not just about gaining knowledge; it's about embracing a mindset that fuels resilience, innovation and a commitment to continuous growth. Whether you are an established entrepreneur or just starting your business, this exercise is designed to elevate your skills, broaden your perspective, and propel you to unprecedented success.

Prepare to unleash your full potential, cultivate your leadership prowess, and seize the limitless possibilities that await you as you embark on this challenging exercise.

Your journey to business excellence starts here - let's empower your vision and ride together!

EXERCISE PLAN

CULTIVATING CONSISTENT FINANCIAL HABITS

Week 1-2: Tracking Your Daily Spending

- Set up a dedicated notebook or a smartphone app to record every expense you make, no matter how small.
- Review your spending patterns at the end of each week. Are there any surprises? Identify areas where you could potentially cut back.

Week 3-4: Creating a Budget

- Design a budget that allocates your income into categories like savings, bills, groceries, entertainment, etc.
- Stick to your budget and track your progress. Adjust as needed and find creative ways to save more.

Week 5-6: Setting Up Automatic Savings

- Open a separate savings account if you don't already have one.
- Set up an automatic transfer to this account every time you receive your paycheck.

Week 7-8: The 24-Hour Rule

- For non-essential purchases, practice the "24-hour rule." Wait 24 hours before buying something to see if you still want it.
- Use this time to evaluate whether the purchase aligns with your financial goals.

Week 9-10: Small Changes, Big Impact

- Identify one daily expense that you could easily reduce, such as bringing your own lunch instead of eating out.
- Commit to making this change for the next month and track the money you save.

Week 11-12: Savings Challenge

- Challenge yourself to save a specific amount of money over the next month.
- Look for creative ways to cut back on unnecessary expenses to reach your goal.

Week 13-14: Debt Reduction Strategy

- If you have existing debt, create a plan to pay it off more aggressively.
- Explore strategies like the debt snowball or debt avalanche method to accelerate your progress.

Week 15-16: Review and Adjust

- Review your progress over the past few months. What habits have you successfully cultivated?
- Adjust your financial habits and goals as needed based on your experience.

Week 17-18: Focus on a Long-Term Goal

- Identify a significant long-term financial goal, such as buying a house or starting a business.
- Break down this goal into smaller, actionable steps and begin working on them consistently.

Week 19-20: Celebrate Your Achievements

- Reflect on the financial habits you've developed and the progress you've made.
- Celebrate your achievements, no matter how small. Treat yourself to something special as a reward for your dedication.

Remember, the key to success is consistency. Each week builds on the previous one, and over time, these small changes will lead to significant financial growth and victory.

Stay committed, and don't be afraid to seek support or advice when needed.

CONCLUSION

In "Achieving Financial Confidence: Overcoming Challenges and Staying Focused," you've embarked on a transformative journey to fortify your resilience, master emotional intelligence, and cultivate unwavering determination in your pursuit of financial success. The tools and insights you've gained throughout this chapter empower you to face adversity with newfound strength, make rational decisions in the face of uncertainty, and build an unbreakable foundation for your financial well-being.

Remember, your path to financial confidence is not linear; it's a dynamic and evolving process. Embrace the art of resilience as you navigate unexpected twists and turns, leveraging each challenge as an opportunity to grow and learn. Harness the power of emotional intelligence to forge a harmonious relationship with your finances, making choices that align with your long-term aspirations.

As you cultivate consistent habits, automate your finances, and stay committed to your goals, you're creating a roadmap to enduring success. The compound effect of these small actions will lead to significant gains, propelling you closer to the financial future you envision.

Celebrate your achievements, no matter how small, for they are the building blocks of your ultimate triumph. A vision board will keep your dreams vividly alive, while the support of a financial advisor or a community of like-minded individuals will amplify your motivation and propel you towards new heights.

Your financial journey is an ongoing endeavor, and with each step, you're rewriting your financial narrative. So, continue to embrace the journey with confidence, courage, and determination.

As you move forward, always remember the words of wisdom:

"Forget The Glass Ceiling.

Build A Glass Empire."

In the upcoming chapters, we'll delve deeper into advanced financial strategies, strategic investments, and wealth-building tactics. Get ready to elevate your financial acumen and unlock the full potential of your financial brilliance. Your path to lasting financial empowerment has just begun, and the possibilities are limitless.

Next Steps: Stay tuned for our exploration of advanced financial strategies and wealth-building techniques in the following chapters. Your continued dedication and commitment will propel you towards the pinnacle of financial success.

With unwavering determination and the knowledge you've gained, you're well on your way to unleashing your financial brilliance and building a legacy of abundance and empowerment.

Remember, the journey continues, and your financial destiny is within your grasp. Onward to new horizons!

"Unlock your potential, ignite your possibilities, and conquer your financial world."

CHAPTER 5
MASTERING WEALTH-BUILDING STRATEGIES

In the ever-evolving landscape of financial empowerment, your journey continues to soar. With each step, you're building a solid foundation of knowledge, resilience, and determination. Now, as we dive into Chapter 5, get ready to unlock the doors to mastering wealth-building strategies that will take your financial brilliance to unprecedented heights.

This chapter is designed to equip you with a comprehensive toolkit of wealth-building techniques that will amplify your financial potential. From strategic investments that generate passive income to innovative approaches for optimizing your savings, you're about to embark on a thrilling expedition into the realm of financial mastery.

Throughout these pages, we'll delve into the art of wealth creation, exploring concepts that go beyond mere money management. You'll discover how to leverage your existing resources, identify opportunities in emerging markets, and harness the power of compound growth to multiply your wealth. Whether you're a seasoned investor or just beginning your wealth-building journey, this chapter will provide actionable insights to propel you forward.

Get ready to explore avenues for diversification, navigate the world of real estate and stock markets, and embrace alternative investment vehicles that align with your financial objectives. Our journey together will unveil the secrets of creating, growing, and preserving wealth, empowering you to make informed decisions and secure a prosperous future.

As you turn the pages of Chapter 5, remember that every lesson, every strategy, and every piece of wisdom is a stepping stone towards your financial brilliance. Get ready to embrace new horizons, expand your financial acumen, and master the art of wealth-building. Your financial destiny is waiting, and the next chapter is your guide to claiming it with unwavering confidence.

So, let's embark on this exhilarating voyage together and pave the way for a future defined by financial abundance and empowerment. As you delve into the pages ahead, keep in mind that each insight, each strategy, and each decision has the potential to shape your financial legacy.

Get ready to unleash the full extent of your financial brilliance in Chapter 5: Mastering Wealth-Building Strategies. The journey continues, and the possibilities are boundless.

"Empower your wealth, ignite your prosperity, and sculpt your financial empire."

Section 1

The Art of Diversification

- Unlocking the Power of Diversification -

Diversification is not merely a strategy; it's a philosophy that safeguards your financial journey. We'll dive deep into the art of spreading your investments across different asset classes, unlocking a powerful approach that can fortify your financial foundation. Diversification goes beyond just avoiding putting all your eggs in one basket; it's about strategically aligning your investments to weather the storms and capitalize on the sunny days of the market.

Imagine your investment portfolio as a beautifully orchestrated symphony, where each instrument plays a unique role to create a harmonious melody. Similarly, diversification involves selecting a mix of asset classes, each with its own risk and return profile, to create a well-balanced and resilient portfolio.

We'll guide you through the process of constructing a diversified portfolio that minimizes risk while aiming for optimal returns. From traditional investments like stocks and bonds, which provide stability and income, to more unconventional options like real estate and alternative investments, you'll gain a comprehensive understanding of how to create a tapestry of investments that work in harmony.

Diversification isn't about trying to predict the future; it's about preparing for the unknown. Just as a skilled sailor adjusts their sails to navigate varying wind conditions, you'll learn to adapt your portfolio to changing market dynamics. We'll provide real-life examples of how diversification has protected investors during turbulent times and positioned them to seize opportunities when markets thrive.

By embracing the power of diversification, you'll be equipped to confidently steer your financial ship through market fluctuations. Your investment choices will be rooted in a strategic approach that considers both short-term uncertainties and long-term aspirations. As you embark on this journey, remember that diversification isn't a one-time event; it's an ongoing commitment to your financial success.

Prepare to unlock a world of financial possibilities as we navigate the intricacies of diversification and empower you to build a resilient and prosperous future.

Learn how to construct a diversified portfolio that withstands market volatility and propels your wealth forward.

Imagine you're building a robust and dynamic puzzle, one piece at a time. Each piece represents a different type of investment – stocks, bonds, real estate, and more. As you carefully select and place each piece, you're not just creating a beautiful picture, but a masterpiece of financial security.

Just like a skilled chef combines various ingredients to create a delicious and balanced dish, you'll learn to blend different investment assets to craft a diversified portfolio. This portfolio becomes your shield against the unpredictable winds of market volatility, allowing you to navigate through turbulent times while maintaining your financial course.

Think of diversification as your secret recipe for financial success. It's like planting a diverse garden – some plants thrive in the sun, others in the shade. By spreading your investments across various asset classes, you're ensuring that your financial garden can weather different economic climates and bloom in all seasons.

Imagine you're a skilled pilot navigating through changing weather patterns. A diversified portfolio acts as your navigation system, helping you make adjustments to your financial altitude and direction as market conditions shift. It's not about avoiding turbulence; it's about having the tools and strategies to navigate through it smoothly.

Just as a ship relies on a balanced distribution of weight to sail smoothly, a diversified portfolio distributes risk and reward across different investments. This balance is what propels your wealth forward, allowing you to capture opportunities and achieve your financial goals with confidence.

So, get ready to become the architect of your financial destiny. Through the art of diversification, you'll construct a portfolio that stands strong in the face of uncertainty and propels your wealth forward on a journey of financial growth and prosperity.

- The art of spreading your investments across different asset classes, minimizing risk, and maximizing potential returns.

Picture this: you're a skilled conductor leading a symphony orchestra. Each instrument represents a different asset class – strings, woodwinds, brass, and percussion. As you expertly guide each section, the harmonious blend of sounds creates a masterpiece that resonates with both depth and brilliance.

In the financial world, diversification is your conductor's baton. It's the art of orchestrating your investments across various asset classes, each playing its unique role in your financial composition. Just as a symphony's beauty emerges from the collaboration of diverse instruments, your investment portfolio flourishes when different assets come together in harmony.

Imagine you're a seasoned chef preparing a gourmet feast. You carefully select a variety of ingredients – vegetables, meats, spices, and sauces – to craft a balanced and flavorful dish. Diversification follows a similar principle. By allocating your resources across different assets like stocks, bonds, real estate, and more, you create a recipe for financial success that balances risk and reward.

Think of your investment portfolio as a garden. Each plant represents a different asset class, and you, the diligent gardener, ensure that each plant gets the right amount of sunlight, water, and care. Some plants may thrive in certain conditions while others excel elsewhere. Through diversification, you're cultivating a resilient financial garden that can weather various market conditions.

Consider a seasoned captain steering a ship through unpredictable seas. The ship's stability comes from its balanced design and weight distribution. Similarly, a diversified portfolio distributes risk and opportunity, allowing you to navigate the vast ocean of financial markets with confidence. It's like having multiple sails to catch different winds, propelling you toward your financial destination.

Just as a skilled artist blends different colors to create a captivating painting, diversification allows you to blend different asset classes to create a masterpiece of financial security. By spreading your investments, you minimize the impact of any one asset's poor performance, while maximizing the potential for overall returns. It's a carefully crafted strategy that combines the elements of risk and reward into a harmonious financial symphony.

So, welcome to the world of diversified investing – where the art of spreading your investments across different asset classes is your secret to minimizing risk and unlocking the potential for remarkable returns. Just as a conductor, a chef, a gardener, or a captain uses their expertise to create something extraordinary, you too can create a financial masterpiece through the power of diversification.

- Learn to adapt your portfolio to changing market dynamics

Imagine you're a skilled surfer riding the waves of the ocean. Just as you adjust your balance and position on the board to match the changing currents, diversification enables you to adapt your investment portfolio to the shifting tides of the market. When economic storms arise, your diversified approach acts as a stabilizing force, helping you stay afloat even in choppy waters. Conversely, during periods of market exuberance, your diversified assets act as sails, harnessing the wind's energy and propelling your financial journey forward.

Take the case of a savvy investor named Sarah. Sarah's diversified portfolio includes a mix of stocks, bonds, and real estate investments. During a sudden economic downturn, while stock prices plummeted, her bonds and real estate holdings held steady. This diversification shielded a portion of her wealth from the market turmoil. As markets recovered and real estate values surged, Sarah's strategic allocation allowed her to capture gains and balance out the overall performance of her portfolio.

Consider the story of Alexia, an astute investor who diversified his investments across various sectors. When a specific industry faced a downturn due to regulatory changes, Alexia's portfolio was only minimally affected because his other investments remained resilient. This diversification strategy allowed him to weather the storm in one area while capitalizing on growth in others.

Imagine a scenario where you're building a puzzle. Each piece represents a different asset class – stocks, bonds, real estate, and more. Just as the pieces come together to create a complete picture, diversification pieces together your investments to create a resilient and balanced portfolio. If one piece doesn't fit perfectly, the entire picture isn't compromised. Instead, the overall image remains intact and compelling.

Think about a seasoned farmer planting a diverse range of crops. While some crops may face challenges due to weather conditions or pests, others flourish and ensure a bountiful harvest. Similarly, a diversified portfolio allows you to plant various financial "crops" that respond differently to market conditions. This approach helps safeguard your investments from unforeseen challenges while reaping the rewards of those that thrive.

In essence, diversification is like having a toolbox filled with different tools. Just as a skilled craftsperson selects the right tool for each task, a diversified investor allocates resources to different asset classes based on market conditions. This adaptability empowers you to weather storms, seize opportunities, and navigate the ever-changing landscape of financial markets. So, as you embark on the journey of diversification, remember that you're equipping yourself with the ability to adapt and thrive. By learning to adjust your portfolio to changing market dynamics, you'll join the ranks of investors who have harnessed the power of diversification to protect their wealth and capitalize on growth, even in the most uncertain times.

- Exploring Emerging Markets –

Imagine stepping onto a vast and uncharted terrain, where the soil is rich with possibilities waiting to be cultivated. This is the realm of emerging markets, where innovation and growth converge to create opportunities that can reshape the financial landscape. In this section, we'll be your guides on this exciting journey, equipping you with the knowledge and tools to navigate these fertile grounds.

Just as explorers of old set sail in search of new lands and treasures, you too can set your sights on emerging trends, industries, and regions that hold the promise of substantial returns. Picture yourself as a modern-day explorer, armed with a map of potential opportunities and a compass of strategic insight.

One such terrain to explore is the realm of technological innovation. The digital age has opened up a world of possibilities, from groundbreaking advancements in artificial intelligence and blockchain to disruptive technologies that reshape industries. Consider the case of a visionary investor who recognized the potential of electric vehicles before they became mainstream. By investing in emerging electric vehicle companies and associated technologies, this investor positioned themselves at the forefront of a transformative movement, reaping significant rewards as the market embraced these innovations.

Another promising landscape to traverse is the realm of renewable energy. As the world shifts towards sustainable practices, renewable energy sources like solar, wind, and hydroelectric power are gaining momentum. Imagine being an early adopter in this sector, capitalizing on the global push towards cleaner energy solutions. By identifying emerging companies and technologies in renewable energy, you have the chance to not only contribute to a greener future but also reap the benefits of a rapidly expanding market.

Global markets themselves are also rich terrain for exploration. As economies evolve and new trade routes emerge, emerging markets can offer exceptional growth potential. Picture yourself diversifying your portfolio to include investments in regions experiencing rapid economic development. Through careful research and strategic allocation, you can tap into the growth trajectories of countries that were once considered untapped markets.

Just as a gardener nurtures young plants to maturity, nurturing investments in emerging markets requires patience and strategic care. It involves conducting thorough research, assessing risks, and staying attuned to shifting trends. The art of exploring emerging markets lies in your ability to discern the budding opportunities from the temporary fads, and the lasting transformations from the passing novelties.

In the realm of finance, as in exploration, knowledge is your most valuable compass. By gaining insights into emerging trends and industries, you can chart a course towards the frontiers of financial growth. As you embark on this exploration of emerging markets, remember that you are harnessing the power of foresight and innovation, positioning yourself to reap the rewards of discovering untapped potential.

So, prepare to embark on this exciting journey, armed with the tools to identify and seize opportunities in emerging markets. As you navigate this terrain, keep in mind that just as explorers of old changed the course of history, your exploration of emerging markets has the potential to shape your financial future in ways you've never imagined.

As you venture into the world of emerging markets, consider the story of Maria, a savvy investor with an eye for untapped potential. Maria recognized the rising demand for sustainable products and technologies, leading her to explore the realm of renewable energy. By investing in innovative solar energy companies at an early stage, Maria not only aligned her portfolio with her values but also reaped substantial financial gains as the renewable energy sector flourished.

Another example to draw inspiration from is the journey of Jenny, a forward-thinking investor who saw the potential of blockchain technology before it became a mainstream buzzword. Jenny's exploration of emerging markets led him to invest in blockchain startups and cryptocurrencies.

As blockchain applications expanded beyond cryptocurrency, Jenny's investments proved to be visionary, positioning her at the forefront of a transformative technological wave.
The concept of exploring emerging markets extends beyond industries; it also encompasses regions that are experiencing rapid growth and development. Imagine an investor like Alicia, who identified the emerging middle class in certain developing countries. By strategically investing in businesses catering to this expanding market, Alicia not only participated in these economies' upward trajectory but also diversified his portfolio to capture unique opportunities.

It's important to note that exploration doesn't guarantee instant success. Just as early explorers faced challenges and uncertainties, your journey into emerging markets may encounter bumps along the way. The key lies in diligent research, staying informed about global trends, and adapting your strategies as the landscape evolves.

As you embark on this journey, consider creating a diversified approach that combines your existing investments with carefully selected opportunities in emerging markets. Much like a seasoned explorer diversifies their route to avoid risks, you can minimize potential downsides while maximizing your chances of success.

Remember that exploration requires a mix of curiosity, courage, and calculated risk-taking. Just as explorers of old set sail with a sense of adventure, you too can approach emerging markets with an open mind and a willingness to embrace the unknown. The path you tread may not have been paved before, but it is illuminated by the potential for significant financial growth and a lasting impact on your financial future.

So, set sail on this exhilarating expedition armed with the tools to identify and seize opportunities in emerging markets. As you navigate uncharted waters and discover new horizons, remember that your journey has the power to shape your financial destiny, leaving a legacy of foresight, innovation, and prosperity for generations to come.

Section 2
Navigating the Financial Markets

Welcome to the intricate world of financial markets, where opportunities abound and strategies are the compass to navigate the ever-changing landscape. In this section, we will equip you with the knowledge and insights to master the art of strategic investing, ensuring that your financial journey is guided by informed decisions and a clear sense of purpose.

- Navigating the Stock Market

Imagine yourself as a skilled sailor, navigating the vast ocean of stocks, bonds, and other securities. Just as a captain studies the stars and currents to chart the best course, you'll learn how to analyze market trends, understand company valuations, and decipher financial indicators to make strategic investment choices.

We'll demystify the terminology and concepts that define the stock market, from equities and indices to market volatility and trading strategies. Whether you're a seasoned investor or new to the world of stocks, this section will provide you with the tools to confidently navigate the stock market and make investment decisions aligned with your goals.

Embarking on the journey of mastering wealth-building strategies requires us to delve into the heart of one of the most dynamic and influential aspects of the financial world: the stock market. In this section, we will demystify the terminology and concepts that define the stock market, unraveling its complexities and empowering you with a deep understanding of its inner workings.

Imagine the stock market as a vibrant tapestry woven with threads of equities, indices, market volatility, and trading strategies. At first glance, this tapestry might seem intricate and bewildering, but fear not – we're here to guide you step by step, unraveling each thread to reveal the masterpiece that is the stock market.

Equities, often referred to as stocks, are the cornerstone of the stock market. They represent ownership in a company and offer a slice of its potential profits and risks. Think of equities as your entry ticket to the world of corporate ownership, where you become a shareholder and participate in a company's growth and success.

Indices, on the other hand, act as barometers that measure the pulse of the stock market. Just as a weather vane indicates wind direction, market indices such as the S&P 500 or the Dow Jones Industrial Average provide insights into the performance of specific groups of stocks. These indices reflect the collective sentiment of investors and offer valuable clues about market trends and directions.

Market volatility, often likened to the ebb and flow of ocean waves, refers to the rapid and unpredictable fluctuations in stock prices. Understanding market volatility is crucial, as it can impact your investment decisions and risk tolerance. We will equip you with tools to navigate this volatility, helping you make informed choices even when the financial waters become choppy.

Trading strategies are the compasses that guide investors through the stock market's vast expanse. Much like a skilled navigator chooses the optimal route through open waters, you'll learn about various trading approaches that cater to different goals and timeframes. Whether you're drawn to day trading, swing trading, or long-term investing, we will demystify these strategies, allowing you to embark on your stock market journey with confidence.

Imagine the stock market as a language, and each of these terms as words and phrases that, when understood, enable you to engage in meaningful conversations. We will provide you with a comprehensive glossary, allowing you to decipher the language of the stock market and converse fluently with fellow investors and financial experts.

Just as a traveler prepares for an overseas adventure by learning the local customs and phrases, you'll be fully equipped to navigate the intricacies of the stock market. No longer will terms like "bull market" and "bear market" be mysterious or intimidating – you'll understand their nuances and implications, making informed decisions that align with your financial objectives.

By demystifying these concepts, we're not just providing you with knowledge; we're bestowing upon you the power to engage with the stock market on your terms. With each concept you grasp, you're building a foundation of financial acumen that will serve you throughout your investment journey. The stock market, once a realm shrouded in mystery, will become a realm of opportunity and potential, ready for you to explore and conquer.

As you embrace the knowledge gained in this section, remember that you're stepping into a world where understanding breeds confidence and empowerment. Just as a linguist becomes proficient in a foreign language, you'll become fluent in the language of the stock market, paving the way for meaningful interactions and strategic decisions. Get ready to demystify, engage, and thrive in the vibrant arena of the stock market – a realm where your financial brilliance is destined to shine.

In the dynamic and ever-evolving landscape of wealth creation, the ability to navigate the intricacies of the financial markets is an invaluable skill. As you embark on the journey of mastering wealth-building strategies, one of the fundamental pillars is the art of analyzing market trends, deciphering financial indicators, and understanding company valuations.

Picture yourself as a seasoned explorer embarking on a quest for hidden treasures. In the realm of investing, these treasures are the opportunities that lie within the financial markets. To uncover these opportunities and make informed decisions, you need a reliable compass, a tool that helps you understand the currents and tides of market trends.

Market trends are like the pulse of the financial world, indicating the ebb and flow of investor sentiment, economic conditions, and industry dynamics. By learning to analyze these trends, you gain the ability to anticipate potential shifts and make proactive investment choices. Imagine you're a weathered sailor, reading the signs of the sky to predict changing weather patterns. Similarly, market trend analysis empowers you to anticipate potential shifts and adjust your financial course accordingly.

Understanding company valuations is like

deciphering the language of financial storytelling. Just as a skilled detective interprets clues to solve a mystery, you'll delve into a company's financial statements and performance metrics to uncover its true value. This skill is your magnifying glass, helping you separate promising investment opportunities from overhyped ventures. You'll learn to assess a company's revenue, earnings, assets, and liabilities – all critical pieces of the valuation puzzle.

Financial indicators serve as your navigational charts in the vast ocean of investing. These indicators are like signposts that provide insights into a company's health, performance, and growth potential. Imagine you're an expert map reader, interpreting symbols and markers to plot your course. Similarly, financial indicators guide you in evaluating a company's financial stability, profitability, and overall trajectory.

By mastering the art of analyzing market trends, understanding company valuations, and deciphering financial indicators, you become a skilled investor equipped to make strategic choices that align with your financial goals. You'll be able to identify opportunities that others might overlook, anticipate market shifts, and make well-informed decisions that have the potential to yield substantial returns.

Imagine you're an architect, meticulously designing the blueprint for a thriving financial future. Your understanding of market trends, company valuations, and financial indicators shapes the foundation upon which your investment decisions are built. Just as an architect envisions a structure's form and function, you'll develop a clear vision of your investment strategy, ensuring that each choice contributes to your overall financial brilliance.

In essence, learning to analyze market trends, understand company valuations, and decipher financial indicators is like acquiring a set of tools that empower you to sculpt your financial destiny. With each insight you gain, you're adding another instrument to your toolkit, honing your ability to make strategic investment choices that resonate with your aspirations.

As you progress on this enlightening journey, remember that these skills are not reserved for financial experts alone. They are accessible to you, an ambitious and empowered individual who is dedicated to unlocking the full potential of their financial brilliance. The path may seem intricate, but with each step you take, you're enhancing your ability to seize opportunities, mitigate risks, and shape a future that is defined by financial prosperity and fulfillment.

In the vast expanse of the financial world, the stock market stands as a bustling marketplace where fortunes are made and opportunities abound. As we delve deeper into the realm of mastering wealth-building strategies, you will be equipped with a robust set of tools that empower you to confidently navigate the stock market and make investment decisions that are precisely aligned with your unique goals.

Imagine the stock market as a dynamic ecosystem, teeming with a diverse array of companies, industries, and investment opportunities. Just as a skilled ecologist studies the interactions between species in an ecosystem, you will learn to analyze the intricate relationships between companies, market sectors, and economic forces. This knowledge is your key to unlocking the potential of the stock market and making choices that resonate with your financial aspirations.

At the heart of your journey lies the ability to decipher the complex language of stocks, bonds, mutual funds, and exchange-traded funds (ETFs). Think of these as the instruments of the stock market, each with its distinct melody. We will guide you through understanding the notes, rhythms, and harmonies of these financial instruments, allowing you to compose a symphony of investments that suits your risk tolerance, timeline, and goals.

Just as a seasoned astronomer gazes at the night sky to decipher the movements of celestial bodies, you'll delve into the world of market indices and company valuations. These indicators act as your celestial maps, guiding you through the vast constellations of financial data. You will learn to interpret these signals, gaining insights into the performance of companies and market sectors. This knowledge enables you to make informed decisions, akin to a seasoned sailor navigating through uncharted waters.

As you venture further, the distinction between value and growth investing will come into focus. Much like an art connoisseur discerns between different styles and periods, you'll explore the nuances of these investment philosophies. Value investing involves seeking out undervalued companies with strong fundamentals, while growth investing focuses on companies with high potential for future expansion. Your understanding of these concepts will empower you to tailor your investment strategy to your preferences and objectives.

Visualize yourself as a master strategist, crafting a roadmap that aligns with your financial goals. With each tool you acquire, you're building a versatile toolkit that allows you to adapt to changing market conditions, seize opportunities, and steer clear of pitfalls. You'll be equipped to analyze financial statements, evaluate market trends, and make decisions that reflect your vision of financial success.

Just as a skilled navigator charts a course through treacherous waters, you'll learn to assess risk and reward, evaluate market volatility, and adjust your investment portfolio as needed. Your newfound knowledge will empower you to make investment choices that stand firm even in the face of market turbulence, much like a well-built ship that withstands stormy seas.

By providing you with these tools, we're not merely imparting knowledge; we're arming you with a strategic advantage that enables you to participate in the stock market with confidence. The journey ahead will be one of exploration, discovery, and continuous learning. Just as a seasoned explorer navigates through uncharted territories, you'll navigate the dynamic landscape of the stock market, uncovering hidden gems and making choices that amplify your financial brilliance.

As you embrace these tools, remember that you're not alone on this journey. Our guidance and insights will serve as your compass, helping you steer toward your financial goals with precision. With each decision you make, you're not just investing in stocks – you're investing in your own financial empowerment, forging a path toward a future defined by prosperity and abundance.

- Value vs. Growth

As you set sail in the world of stocks, you'll encounter two distinct approaches – value investing and growth investing. Picture these as two different routes to the same destination: financial prosperity. We'll delve into the strategies behind each approach, helping you understand when to seek undervalued gems or capitalize on high-growth opportunities.

Through real-world examples and case studies, you'll gain the expertise to identify stocks that align with your investment philosophy. Just as a skilled hiker chooses different paths depending on the terrain, you'll learn to tailor your investment strategy based on your risk tolerance and financial aspirations.

Embarking on your stock market journey is akin to setting sail on a vast and dynamic sea of opportunities. As you navigate this financial ocean, you'll soon encounter two distinct approaches that will shape your voyage – value investing and growth investing. Think of these approaches as divergent paths, each leading to the same destination: the shores of financial prosperity. In this section, we will be your navigators, guiding you through the strategies that underpin each approach, empowering you to make informed decisions that align with your unique investment goals.

Imagine value investing as a scenic route through uncharted landscapes, where hidden treasures await discovery. This approach involves seeking out stocks that the market has undervalued, presenting a chance to acquire assets at a discount. Think of it as stumbling upon a hidden gem at a flea market – an item that others may have overlooked, but one that holds immense potential. We will equip you with the tools to identify these undervalued stocks, enabling you to make strategic investments that have the potential to yield substantial returns.

On the other hand, growth investing is like setting sail on a high-speed vessel, aiming to reach your destination as quickly as possible. This approach involves targeting companies that are poised for rapid expansion and high earnings growth. Picture a young sapling growing into a towering tree – growth investing focuses on companies that are in their growth phase, with the potential to significantly increase their market value over time.
We will guide you through the process of identifying these high-growth opportunities,

allowing you to capitalize on companies that are on a trajectory to achieve remarkable success.

Through the use of real-world examples and insightful case studies, you'll gain the expertise to differentiate between these two approaches and select the one that resonates with your investment philosophy. Just as a skilled mountaineer chooses different routes based on the terrain and personal preferences, you'll learn to tailor your investment strategy to match your risk tolerance, financial aspirations, and time horizon.

Consider the story of Julia, a value investor who recognized the potential of a well-established company trading below its intrinsic value. By investing in this undervalued stock, Julia was able to capitalize on its subsequent rise in market price, turning her initial investment into a substantial gain.

On the other hand, envision Tom, a growth investor who identified a small tech startup with groundbreaking innovations.Recognizing its potential for explosive growth, Tom invested early and reaped substantial rewards as the company's stock soared in value.

As you embark on your journey through the realms of value and growth investing, keep in mind that these approaches are not mutually exclusive. Just as a seasoned sailor adjusts their sails to navigate changing winds, you'll have the flexibility to incorporate elements of both approaches into your investment strategy.

Ultimately, the choice between value and growth investing hinges on your individual preferences and financial objectives. We will empower you with the knowledge to make strategic decisions, ensuring that your investment choices are aligned with your goals.

So, get ready to navigate the world of stocks with a compass calibrated to the principles of value and growth investing. Like a skilled navigator charting a course through uncharted waters, you'll have the expertise to steer your investment ship towards success. As you explore these distinct approaches, remember that each path offers its own set of opportunities and rewards. Your journey through the stock market is an expedition of discovery, empowerment, and financial growth – an expedition that promises to leave an indelible mark on your financial brilliance.

- Navigating the Bond Market

Imagine stepping into a world of financial instruments known as bonds – where companies and governments raise capital by issuing debt securities. This section will guide you through the bond market, explaining the intricacies of bond types, interest rates, and yield curves.

You'll learn to assess the risk and potential returns of different bonds, understanding how changes in interest rates impact bond prices. Much like a craftsperson selecting the right tool for the job, you'll be empowered to choose bonds that align with your investment goals, whether it's stability, income, or growth.

Embark on a journey into the intricate realm of the bond market, a world of financial instruments where companies and governments harness the power of debt to raise capital. Picture yourself as an astute observer, stepping into a bustling marketplace where bonds are bought and sold, each one representing a unique opportunity for both issuers and investors.

Think of bonds as intricate financial agreements, where the issuer borrows funds from investors and promises to repay the principal amount along with periodic interest payments. As you delve into this section, you're equipped with a lantern of knowledge that will illuminate the complexities of bond types, interest rates, and yield curves.

Imagine navigating through a vast landscape of bond varieties, each with its distinct features and potential benefits. Government bonds, for instance, are akin to rock-solid foundations that provide stability and security to investors. On the other hand, corporate bonds offer a blend of risk and reward, allowing you to tap into the growth potential of companies while enjoying regular interest income.

As you tread further into the bond market, the concept of interest rates takes center stage. Just as the tides of the ocean rise and fall, interest rates ebb and flow, shaping the dynamics of bond prices. Your journey through this terrain will empower you to decipher the relationship between interest rates and bond values, understanding how fluctuations in rates impact the attractiveness of different bonds.

Now, envision a landscape of yield curves, a graphical representation of the interest rates on bonds of varying maturities. Like a cartographer charting uncharted territories, you'll learn to interpret yield curves, gaining insights into market expectations and potential economic trends. These curves become your navigational tools, guiding you toward bonds that align with your investment objectives.

Consider the story of Emily, a discerning investor who ventured into the bond market. By selecting government bonds with lower yields but higher stability, Emily safeguarded her investment capital during times of market uncertainty. Her prudent choice demonstrated how bonds can provide a sheltered harbor amidst financial storms.

As you continue your expedition, imagine yourself as a skilled craftsman selecting the right tool for a specific task. Similarly, you'll become adept at choosing bonds that match your investment goals. Seeking stability? Government bonds may be your go-to option. Pursuing income? Corporate bonds could fit the bill. Craving growth potential? High-yield bonds might capture your attention.

Just as a seasoned sailor adjusts their sails to navigate changing winds, you'll master the art of evaluating risks and potential returns to make informed decisions in the bond market. Your journey will be enriched with insights into how bonds can complement your existing investment portfolio, adding layers of diversification and stability.

As you explore the bond market, remember that knowledge is your compass, and understanding the intricacies of bonds allows you to navigate with confidence. By delving into this section, you're arming yourself with the skills to assess bonds like a seasoned connoisseur, making choices that align with your financial aspirations. Whether you're seeking stability, income, or growth, the bonmarket offers a rich tapestry of opportunities for you to explore, and your newfound expertise will be your guide through this captivating landscape.

- Alternative Investments

In your journey through the intricate landscapes of the financial markets, you'll soon come across a fascinating realm known as alternative investments – a world that extends far beyond the familiar territories of traditional stocks and bonds. Consider this journey as a thrilling expedition where you, the intrepid explorer, uncover hidden treasures that promise to add depth, diversity, and potential rewards to your investment journey.

Imagine stepping into this realm of alternative investments, equipped with a lantern of knowledge and a compass of insight. Like a curious adventurer, you're about to unveil a collection of unique opportunities that have the potential to reshape your investment landscape. These opportunities include real estate investment trusts (REITs), commodities, private equity, and hedge funds – each with its own distinct allure and potential for financial growth.

REITs, for instance, are like keys that grant you access to the alluring world of real estate without the responsibilities of property ownership. Think of them as a magical map that guides you through the intricate streets of real estate ventures, allowing you to potentially benefit from rental income and property value appreciation.

Now, picture yourself as a gemologist, exploring the world of commodities – the precious jewels of the investment realm. These tangible assets, ranging from precious metals to energy resources, act as a hedge against market fluctuations and inflation, adding a layer of security to your investment portfolio.

As you continue your expedition, you'll stumble upon the uncharted territory of private equity. This realm resembles a hidden trove of potential riches, offering opportunities to invest in privately held companies that may not be accessible through traditional stock markets. Like a wise explorer, you'll learn the art of due diligence and risk assessment as you consider these exclusive opportunities.

Finally, venture into the mysterious world of hedge funds – a place where strategic maneuvering and financial agility are the keys to success. These professionally managed funds employ a range of strategies to potentially generate returns that are not necessarily tied to the performance of traditional markets.

As your guides through this realm, we'll provide you with a detailed map that outlines the benefits and potential pitfalls of these alternative investment avenues. You'll gain insights into how they can complement and diversify your existing portfolio, and how they fit within your overall investment strategy.

Consider the story of Rachel, an astute investor who diversified her portfolio by investing in commodities. During a period of economic uncertainty, her investments in precious metals acted as a stabilizing force, protecting her wealth from the volatility of traditional markets.

Similarly, envision Mark, who explored the realm of private equity and seized an opportunity to invest in an emerging technology startup. His foresight and strategic decision-making led him to reap significant rewards as the startup grew and flourished.

Navigating the world of alternative investments requires both a sense of adventure and a grasp of insight. You, the explorer, will be empowered to make informed decisions as you uncover each unique opportunity. By understanding the intricacies of alternative investments, you'll be equipped to enhance your investment strategy and create a portfolio that reflects both diversity and potential growth.

So, prepare to set foot in this captivating realm, armed with knowledge and curiosity. Your journey into alternative investments is a testament to your dedication to financial excellence and your willingness to venture beyond the familiar to unlock new dimensions of financial brilliance. As you explore these pathways, remember that you're not just investing – you're embarking on a quest to expand your financial horizons and unlock the hidden treasures that await your discovery.

As we conclude our exploration of Section 2, we stand at the threshold of a significant juncture – Chapter 6: Securing Your Financial Legacy. This closing chapter represents the pinnacle of our journey through the intricate landscapes of investment strategies, market dynamics, and alternative avenues.

Throughout this section, you've acquired a wealth of insights and tools. You've navigated the complexities of market trends and learned to decipher financial indicators, empowering you to make informed investment decisions. You've gained the confidence to venture into the stock market, armed with an understanding of key concepts and trading strategies. Additionally, you've explored alternative investments, expanding your portfolio's potential and enhancing your overall strategy.

Now, as we prepare to step into the final chapter, envision a new horizon on the horizon – a horizon that encompasses securing your financial legacy. Chapter 6 will guide you through crafting a comprehensive estate plan that ensures the seamless transfer of your wealth, leaving an indelible mark for generations to come. We'll unveil the power of philanthropy, allowing you to make a lasting impact on society that transcends mere financial gains.

Your journey thus far has been transformative, equipping you with the knowledge and tools to navigate the intricate world of finance. As you enter the final stretch of this remarkable expedition, remember that the culmination of your financial brilliance is within reach.

Chapter 6 awaits, poised to reveal the keys to securing your financial legacy – a legacy defined by vision, resilience, and the enduring impact you will leave on the tapestry of time. So, gather your learnings, embrace your newfound expertise, and prepare to embark on the ultimate chapter of your journey – a chapter that holds the promise of shaping a legacy that stands as a beacon of inspiration for generations to come.

CHAPTER 6

SECURING YOUR FINANCIAL LEGACY

Welcome to the culminating chapter of your transformative journey towards financial brilliance. In Chapter 6, we delve into the realm of securing your financial legacy – a realm where your efforts transcend time, leaving an indelible mark on the generations to come. As you immerse yourself in these pages, prepare to uncover the intricacies of estate planning, philanthropy, and the art of leaving a lasting impact on the world.

Section 1
Crafting Your Estate Plan

Estate planning is more than a legal process; it's a legacy you sculpt with precision. In this section, we guide you through the elements of a comprehensive estate plan, from drafting wills and trusts to designating beneficiaries and minimizing estate taxes. Your legacy takes shape as you ensure the seamless transfer of your assets to your loved ones and chosen causes.

- Crafting Your Estate Plan: Guiding You Through Essential Elements

Welcome to the enlightening journey of crafting your estate plan, a cornerstone of securing your financial legacy. In this pivotal section, we are your trusted guides, poised to lead you through the intricate tapestry of estate planning. Our mission is to empower you, ambitious businesswomen, with the knowledge and tools to shape a legacy that endures for generations to come.

Estate planning is a meticulous and purposeful endeavor, far beyond a mere legal process. It is an art that involves the meticulous sculpting of your wishes and aspirations into a tangible plan. With our guidance, you'll master the pivotal components that form the bedrock of an all-encompassing estate plan. Let's explore these essential elements in depth:

1. Drafting Wills and Trusts: Building Your Blueprint for the Future Think of wills and trusts as the architect's blueprint for your financial legacy. We'll navigate you through the process of creating a will that reflects your intentions down to the finest detail. You'll understand how a well-structured trust can safeguard your assets, providing for your loved ones while minimizing complexities.

2. Designating Beneficiaries: Ensuring Your Wishes are Honored Designating beneficiaries is like leaving personalized notes for your loved ones in the book of your life. We'll show you how to assign beneficiaries to your accounts, investments, and assets, ensuring your wishes are honored and a seamless transfer of wealth occurs.

3. Minimizing Estate Taxes: Safeguarding Your Wealth for Future Generations Estate taxes can erode the legacy you've worked tirelessly to build. Our guidance will empower you to employ strategic maneuvers to minimize these taxes, allowing your heirs to inherit a more substantial share of your hard-earned wealth.

Through vivid real-world examples and relatable case studies, you'll gain a profound understanding of the significance of these elements. Just as a skilled artist uses a palette of colors to create a masterpiece, you'll learn how to blend these components harmoniously to craft an estate plan that resonates with your unique values and aspirations.

Our aim is to unravel the complexities, providing you with a clear roadmap to navigate the estate planning landscape. Armed with this knowledge, you'll be able to take charge of your financial destiny with confidence. By securing your legacy through well-structured wills, trusts, and beneficiary designations, you're sowing the seeds for a lasting impact that will stand as a testament to your foresight and dedication.

As you immerse yourself in the art of estate planning, remember that every decision you make is a brushstroke on the canvas of your legacy. With each carefully chosen element, you are crafting a masterpiece that will leave an indelible mark on the generations that follow.

Prepare to journey deeper into the realm of securing your financial legacy, for in the chapters ahead, we will explore further strategies that preserve your wealth and empower you to make a profound impact on the world around you.

"Shape a legacy that echoes through time, a symphony of your wisdom and aspirations."

- Preserving Your Wealth for Future Generations

Explore strategies to preserve your wealth across generations. Learn about the benefits of setting up family trusts, establishing education funds, and ensuring a seamless transition of assets. By mastering these techniques, you create a timeless legacy that nurtures and empowers your heirs for years to come.

Preserving Your Wealth for Future Generations: Nurturing a Timeless Legacy

In the tapestry of your financial brilliance, there lies a chapter dedicated to preserving the wealth you've diligently cultivated. As ambitious businesswomen, you possess the power not only to amass success in the present but to extend its influence across generations. In this section, we embark on a transformative journey that unveils strategies to preserve your wealth, ensuring that its benefits ripple through time, nurturing and empowering those who follow in your footsteps.

1. Setting Up Family Trusts: Weaving a Protective Veil Around Your Legacy

Imagine a family trust as a sturdy vault, sheltering your wealth from the elements of uncertainty. Our exploration begins with the art of setting up family trusts, a strategic move that safeguards your assets while bestowing invaluable benefits. Through these trusts, you gain the power to control the distribution of your wealth, ensure the well-being of your loved ones, and minimize potential tax burdens. As you master the craft of establishing family trusts, you bestow upon your heirs the gift of financial stability, a beacon guiding them through the ever-changing tides of life.

2. Establishing Education Funds: Illuminating Pathways of Knowledge

Education is the cornerstone upon which dreams are built, and as a visionary businesswoman, you understand its significance. Delve into the world of education funds, a potent tool that empowers you to nurture the pursuit of knowledge among your descendants. By creating these funds, you pave the way for future generations to access quality education, fostering their growth and equipping them to stride confidently toward their aspirations. As your legacy flourishes through education, you grant the invaluable gift of enlightenment that transcends time.

3. Ensuring a Seamless Transition of Assets:
    Handing Down Your Wisdom

A seamless transition of assets is akin to passing down a torch of guidance and opportunity. Here, we unravel the intricate threads of inheritance, equipping you with the knowledge to orchestrate a smooth transfer of your wealth. You'll grasp the intricacies of wills, trusts, and beneficiary designations, ensuring that your intentions are honored with precision. As you master these techniques, you create a legacy of continuity, where your heirs can seamlessly step into their roles as custodians of your vision.

Through the mastery of these techniques, you forge a timeless legacy that transcends mere financial wealth. Your wealth becomes a catalyst for empowerment, nurturing future generations and igniting the flames of their ambitions. The impact you make extends beyond dollars and cents – it weaves a narrative of strength, foresight, and unwavering support.

As you delve into these strategies, remember that you are not merely preserving wealth; you are nurturing the potential of those who come after you. Your legacy will stand as a testament to your dedication, a lighthouse guiding your heirs toward their own aspirations.

In the chapters that unfold, we continue to empower you, offering insights into the art of philanthropy and guiding you toward a lasting impact on society. Your journey as an ambitious businesswoman is not confined to the present; it's a symphony of influence that echoes through the corridors of time.

"Preserve your wealth, and in doing so, cultivate a garden of opportunity for the generations that follow."

Section 2

The Art of Philanthropy

Unleashing the Power of Giving: Philanthropy is a force that transcends financial wealth, igniting positive change in the world. Discover the art of giving strategically, from choosing charitable causes that resonate with your values to establishing foundations and endowments. In this section, we unveil the ways philanthropy aligns with your financial goals and empowers you to make a profound impact on society.

Unleashing the Power of Giving: Illuminating a Path of Impact

In the realm of financial brilliance, there exists a transformative force that extends beyond the boundaries of wealth – philanthropy. As ambitious businesswomen, you hold within your hands the power to ignite positive change that reverberates far beyond your individual achievements. This section is an invitation to embark on a journey of purposeful giving, to explore the art of philanthropy in all its dimensions, and to witness the profound impact it can have on both your legacy and the world at large.

1. Beyond Financial Wealth: The Essence of Philanthropy

Philanthropy is not confined to financial resources; it's an embodiment of empathy, a channel for your values, and a testament to your desire to contribute to a better world. It's a force that transcends dollars and cents, reaching into the core of societal needs. In this exploration, you'll understand how philanthropy is a catalyst for change, transforming your financial journey into a legacy of compassion and purpose.

2. Choosing Charitable Causes: Illuminating the Pathway

The art of giving strategically begins with choosing charitable causes that resonate with your passions and values. Just as a painter selects colors to express emotions, you'll learn to identify the causes that ignite your heart. This section empowers you to delve into various sectors – education, healthcare, environment, social justice, and more – and align your giving with the issues that hold personal significance. Your philanthropy becomes a canvas upon which you paint a brighter future.

3. Establishing Foundations and Endowments: Crafting a Lasting Impact

The journey of philanthropy takes a tangible form as we delve into the establishment of foundations and endowments. These structures are not just financial mechanisms; they're vessels of change, allowing you to focus your resources on causes that matter most to you. You'll gain insights into the strategic creation and management of these entities, ensuring that your philanthropic efforts stand the test of time and continue to make a difference for generations to come.

4. Aligning with Financial Goals: Where Philanthropy and Prosperity Converge

Contrary to the notion of separation, philanthropy and financial goals can harmoniously coexist. This section unravels the symbiotic relationship between strategic giving and your financial aspirations. You'll discover how your philanthropic endeavors can align with your broader financial strategy, creating a synergy that not only enriches your legacy but enhances your financial well-being.

5. Empowerment Through Impact: Amplifying Change

The true power of philanthropy lies not only in its capacity to effect change but in its ability to empower. As you immerse yourself in the world of giving, you'll realize the profound impact you can have on society. Your contributions, whether large or small, become seeds of transformation, sprouting into opportunities, progress, and hope. Through strategic giving, you become a driving force behind solutions to global challenges.

A Lasting Legacy: Your Pathway to Transformative Change

As you journey through the art of philanthropy, you're embarking on a pathway of transformative change. Your giving becomes a bridge between your financial brilliance and the betterment of humanity. It's a legacy that will be etched in the annals of time, a testament to your commitment to making the world a better place.

As you reach the culmination of this transformative journey, you stand at the intersection of financial brilliance and purpose-driven impact. The pages of this book have unveiled the art of securing your financial legacy and illuminated the profound possibilities of strategic philanthropy. You, the ambitious businesswomen of today, possess the tools to shape a legacy that transcends time – one that embodies wisdom, compassion, and empowerment. The tapestry of your life's work, woven with dedication and driven by purpose, leaves an indelible mark on the world. As you step forward, embrace the future with the knowledge that your financial brilliance knows no bounds. Let your legacy stand as a beacon, inspiring generations to come, and let your journey serve as a testament to the extraordinary potential within each ambitious soul. With your heart alight with purpose and your path illuminated by the brilliance of your endeavors, you are ready to shape a legacy that transforms lives, uplifts communities, and sparks a brighter tomorrow.

"In the tapestry of life, every thread you weave contributes to a legacy that will be cherished for generations."

AUTHOR'S REFLECTION

A Shared Journey to Financial Success by Ann Bost

In closing, I want to send a sincere note of gratitude and connection. This journey we have embarked on together in "Mapping Your Financial Future" is not just a collection of words on pages; it is a reflection of my unwavering belief in your potential and my commitment to empowering ambitious businesswomen like you. As you've delved into the chapters, absorbing insights, strategies, and advice, know that every tip, concept, and tool shared is rooted in my own journey and experiences. I have walked a path similar to yours, faced challenges and tasted the sweet triumphs of success. It is this very journey that has fueled my passion to equip you with the knowledge and skills you need to chart your own path. My hard work, research, and dedication have all been channeled into creating a resource that not only empowers you financially, but also encourages you to embrace your unique power and potential. I hope "Mapping Your Financial Future" has been an inspiration, a trusted companion, and a beacon of direction as you navigate the complex landscape of finance. Remember, your journey doesn't end there. Just as I have continued to learn, grow and evolve in my own financial endeavors, I encourage you to continue this torch of knowledge and financial brilliance. Your path is lit, your goals are within reach, and your potential is limitless. Thank you for allowing me to be part of your journey. As you move forward, I am thrilled to witness the incredible heights you will reach, the positive impact you will create, and the legacy you will shape for generations to come.

With deep gratitude,

Ann Bost

CONCLUSION

In the brilliant tapestry of your aspirations and achievements, remember that your financial journey is a canvas waiting for your unique strokes of brilliance. As you close the final chapter of "Mapping Your Financial Future," embrace the wisdom you've gained and the empowerment you've cultivated.

From setting clear financial goals that spark your ambitions to mastering the art of investment, navigating markets, and leaving a profound legacy through strategic philanthropy – you've embarked on a transformative expedition. This book has been your compass, guiding you through uncharted financial territories, and now, as you stand on the precipice of new horizons, your potential knows no bounds.

You are not just a spectator in the realm of finance; you are a trailblazer, a visionary, and an embodiment of financial brilliance. Let your journey be a testament to the strength of your dreams, the resilience of your spirit, and the unyielding power of your aspirations.

As you step forward into the world, remember that this is not an end, but a beginning. The knowledge you've gained, the strategies you've honed, and the mindset you've cultivated will accompany you as you shape your destiny.

In the grand symphony of life, you are the conductor of your financial future, orchestrating harmonies of success, growth, and empowerment. Embrace the opportunities that lie ahead, navigate challenges with the prowess you've acquired, and let your financial brilliance illuminate your path.

Your journey as an ambitious businesswoman is a symphony of triumphs, challenges, and unwavering determination. So go forth, with your head held high and your heart aflame with purpose. Your financial future is not just mapped; it's a masterpiece in the making, painted with the colors of your passion, the brushstrokes of your knowledge, and the unwavering belief in your own potential.

Congratulations on reaching this milestone, and may your financial journey continue to shine brightly, inspiring others and leaving an indelible mark on the world. The future is yours to shape, and you are poised to make it a masterpiece of financial brilliance.

ABOUT THE AUTHOR:

Ann Bost

Unlocking Potential Through self conciousness,Mindfulness, Leadership, and Financial Brilliance.

Ann Bost is a visionary author, spiritual business catalyst, and conscious change architect with a career spanning over 20 years. Her journey of self-discovery has led her to explore profound connections between spirituality, leadership, and financial empowerment, making her a guiding light for individuals seeking to unlock their full potential and thrive in today's ever-changing world.

Her First Book: "Authentique: A Journey of Self-Discovery" (Available on Amazon only in French)

In her captivating debut book, Ann shares her personal story of transformation, recounting the trials, triumphs, and pivotal moments that led her to a life infused with mindfulness and purpose. Through her experiences, she illustrates the transformative power of mindfulness, conscious breathing, and self-discovery. Ann's journey, from adversity to authenticity, serves as inspiration to all those seeking meaning and balance in their own lives.

Author of "Voices on Time: Global Women Leaders Speak Out" (Anthology Collection, Volume 1) – Available on Amazon.

Ann joins a diverse group of women leaders from around the world to explore the multifaceted dimensions of time. In this thought-provoking collection, she provides insights into the intersection of time, consciousness, and personal growth. Ann's contributions add depth to a symphony of perspectives, creating a harmonious collection of wisdom.

Author of "Unleash Your Financial Brilliance: 10 Steps for Cultivating a Powerful Financial Mindset". Available on Amazon

Ann's latest work takes readers on a transformative journey into the world of financial empowerment. With this book, she provides readers with a roadmap to cultivate a powerful financial mindset. Drawing on her years of experience, Ann offers practical steps and insights to help individuals take charge of their financial destiny. Her unique approach integrates spirituality into the world of finance, empowering readers to discover their true financial potential.

Ann's mission is crystal clear: to inspire individuals to transcend traditional notions of success. She believes that genuine success is rooted in self-awareness, mindfulness, and harnessing the incredible potential of one's breath and mind. Her work is a beacon of hope and guidance for those on the path of transformation, self-discovery, and financial empowerment.

Join Ann Bost on a journey of self-discovery, mindfulness, and financial brilliance. Explore her books and unlock the transformative power within you.

Thank you for visiting my author's page and learning more about my work. If you're ready to begin your journey towards self-discovery, empowerment, and financial brilliance, I'm here to support you every step of the way. Contact me today to explore how we can work together and create a brighter future filled with success, purpose, and fulfillment.

Ann Bost

www.ingramcontent.com/pod-product-compliance
Lightning Source LLC
Chambersburg PA
CBHW050724260726
48661CB00001B/59